PREPARING TO MOOT

A Step-by-Step Guide to Mooting

SARAH L. COOPER AND
SCARLETT McARDLE

Routledge
Taylor & Francis Group

LONDON AND NEW YORK

First published 2017
by Routledge
2 Park Square, Milton Park, Abingdon, Oxon OX14 4RN

and by Routledge
711 Third Avenue, New York, NY 10017

Routledge is an imprint of the Taylor & Francis Group, an informa business

British Library Cataloguing in Publication Data
A catalogue record for this book is available from the British Library

Library of Congress Cataloging in Publication Data
Names: Cooper, Sarah Lucy, author. | McArdle, Scarlett, author.
Title: Preparing to moot: a step-by-step guide to mooting.
Description: Abingdon, Oxon [UK]; New York: Routledge, 2017. | Includes index.
Identifiers: LCCN 2016054657| ISBN 9781138853140 (hardback) | ISBN 9781138853157 (pbk.)
Subjects: LCSH: Moot courts–Great Britain.
Classification: LCC KD440.A2 C66 2017 | DDC 340.071/41–dc23
LC record available at https://lccn.loc.gov/2016054657

ISBN: 978-1-138-85314-0 (hbk)
ISBN: 978-1-138-85315-7 (pbk)
ISBN: 978-1-315-71334-2 (ebk)

Typeset in Galliard
by Wearset Ltd, Boldon, Tyne and Wear

Printed and bound by CPI Group (UK) Ltd, Croydon, CR0 4YY

DEDICATION

For Graham and Sorcha, who prepared us to moot (and more)...
and for Madeleine who had to listen to every word.

CONTENTS

Foreword   xi

Introduction   xiii

Table of Legal Authorities   xv

Scholarship   xv

Table of Statutes   xvi

Table of Cases   xvi

CHAPTER 1 CRIMINAL LAW   1

Introduction   1

Analysis   2

    The Problem Question   2

    Understanding the Basics of the Problem Question   3

    Summarising the Case   4

    Understanding Your Ground of Appeal   8

    Selecting Your Research Terms   9

    Summary   13

Research   13

    Preliminary Considerations for Researchers   14

    Researching **R v Harper**   14

    Summarising the Relevance of Authorities   19

    Summary   28

Argument Construction   28

    Preliminary Considerations for Constructing a Skeleton Argument   29

    Argument Construction: **R v Harper**   30

    Respondent Skeleton Argument   32

    Editing Draft Skeleton Arguments   37

    Thinking Ahead   41

    Being Critical   41

    Summary   43

Conclusion   43

CONTENTS

CHAPTER 2 TORT LAW   45

Introduction   45

Analysis   46

    The Problem Question   46

    Understanding the Basics of the Problem Question   47

    Summarising the Case   49

    Understanding Your Ground of Appeal   52

    Selecting Your Research Terms   53

    Summary   57

Research   58

    Researching **Live and Loud Ltd v Andrew Jones-Hacker**   58

    Summarising the Relevance of Authorities   63

    Summary   71

Argument Construction   72

    Preliminary Considerations for Constructing a Skeleton Argument   72

    Submissions for the Appellant   72

    Thinking Ahead and Being Critical   81

    Summary   84

Conclusion   84

CHAPTER 3 HUMAN RIGHTS LAW   85

Introduction   85

Analysis   86

    The Problem Question   86

    Understanding the Basics of the Problem Question   87

    Summarising the Case   88

    Understanding Your Ground of Appeal   92

    Selecting Your Research Terms   95

    Summary   98

Research   99

    Researching **Swifter and Handsworth v Daily Herald**   99

    Summarising Your Research   101

    Summary   108

Argument Construction   109

    Submissions for the Appellant   109

    Submissions for the Respondent   112

    Thinking Ahead and Being Critical   116

    Summary   119

Conclusion   120

CHAPTER 4 CONTRACT LAW 121

Introduction 121

Analysis 122

The Problem Question 122

Understanding the Basics of the Problem Question 123

Summarising the Case 125

Understanding Your Ground of Appeal and Appreciating Wider Legal Context 128

Research 131

Researching **Aston v Finn** 132

Case Summaries 133

Summary 137

Argument Construction 138

Submissions for the Appellant 138

Submissions for the Respondent 140

Thinking Ahead and Being Critical 142

Summary 145

Conclusion 145

CHAPTER 5 LAW OF EQUITY 147

Introduction 147

Analysis 148

The Problem Question 148

Understanding the Basics of the Problem Question 149

Summarising the Case 151

Understanding Your Ground of Appeal and Appreciating Wider Legal Context 152

Research 155

Generating Research Terms 155

Generating Authorities 157

Summarising the Relevance of Your Authorities 158

Summary 165

Argument Construction 165

Constructing Your Skeleton Arguments in **Murray v Jokker** 165

Submissions for the Appellant 167

Submissions for the Respondent 169

Thinking Ahead and Being Critical 170

Summary 171

Conclusion 171

CONTENTS

CHAPTER 6 PREPARING FOR ADVOCACY   173

Introduction   173

Presentation Style   173

    Diction   173

    Pace   174

    Voice and Volume   174

    Eye Contact   174

    Personality   175

    Non-verbal Communication   175

Courtroom Etiquette   176

    Attire   176

    Modes of Address   176

    Useful Phrases   177

Using and Pronouncing Authorities   178

    Case Law   178

    Legislation (Domestic)   179

    Law Commission Reports   179

    Journal Articles   180

Using Bundles   180

Handling Difficult Situations   181

    Hostile Judicial Intervention/Not Knowing the Answer to the Judge's Question   181

    Running Out of Time   182

    Judicial Error   182

    Struggling Colleague   182

    Mismatching Arguments   182

    Rule Breaches   183

Conclusion   183

Index   185

FOREWORD

Mooting brought us together. We come from different parts of the world, have different interests and different aspirations; however, we all wanted to be part of something that stood for excellence. All of us got involved with the mooting society at Birmingham City University because we knew it had a reputation for getting the best out of students. Also, while studying would teach us the law, mooting could teach us to be a lawyer.

We were all involved in mooting in a variety of ways, whether through participating directly in moots, or through managerial positions and roles within the mooting society committee. Our various experiences meant we were all able to bring fresh perspectives when Sarah and Scarlett approached us about this project. All of us jumped at the chance to contribute to *Preparing to Moot* because we have all benefitted from being involved with mooting.

Not only has being involved in mooting helped us to deepen the 'obvious' skills of legal research and advocacy, it has gone much further than that. We had the opportunity to network with a wide range of professionals, from lawyers and judges to QCs and Justices of the UK Supreme Court. For some of us, in particular, mooting has helped to develop confidence and the ability to get over fears in presenting an argument, whereas others have mooting to thank for being more astute in their analytical skills. All of us are now able to determine what information is relevant and how to deliver that information persuasively. Now that some of us are working in practice, we realise how important these skills really are. We know that our mooting experiences will inform our careers for years to come.

We would all have loved to have a book like this when we first began mooting. We all felt a little like we had to dive in at the deep end, which is not always a bad thing, but we all would have appreciated having something to help us float! When you first start as a mooter, you do not realise how expansive preparation ought to be. We now know that thorough preparation underpins a good oral argument. Students do not always recognise what is required by 'preparation'. We certainly didn't. We do now. In fact, we have seen how the preparation we have been taught to undertake has tipped the balance in our favour. We would like to help other students to learn this lesson, which is one of the key reasons that we got involved with this book. This book shows some of our development in mooting. Yet, even looking back now, there are things we would change and do differently. In fact, that's one of the biggest things we have all learned: learning is a process and you can always improve and do better.

We will never forget our experience at Birmingham City University. We met some great people, made life-long friends and had the privilege to be taught by great instructors. We all have different people to thank for supporting us during this project and in our studies. In particular, Anna would like to thank Terry Michael and Ali would like to thank his family.

All three of us would like to thank Sarah and Scarlett for inviting us to contribute to this book. Not only are they great teachers of law, they are excellent mentors, wonderful colleagues and great people. We will always be grateful to them for the opportunities and support they have provided. Final thanks go to all our colleagues who worked with us in the mooting society to continue its excellent programme.

We hope our work can play a part in helping other students get started with mooting. We wish all those students the best of luck.

Farukh Bhatti, Anna Hajilari and Ali Kazi
September 2016

INTRODUCTION

Mooting has played, and continues to play, a significant role in our academic lives. Both of us mooted as students and we have no doubt that these experiences assisted in our academic and personal development. As such, when both of us entered academia, we were keen to enable as many students as possible to benefit from the experience of mooting, in the same ways as we had.

We both took over directing the mooting programme at Birmingham City University in 2014, and quickly realised that students tended to overlook the stage of preparing for a moot. Rather, students spent far more time worrying about the oral presentation of their arguments. However, we both knew that a strong oral performance was built upon comprehensive preparation. This is where the idea of *Preparing to Moot* was conceived.

Preparing to Moot guides students through five moot problem questions in criminal law, tort law, human rights law, contract law and the law of equity. Each chapter applies a three-stage process to one of these problems: analysis, research and argument construction. In the sections on analysis, we focus on understanding the features of the problem question, summarising it, appreciating legal context and selecting research terms. In the research sections, we help the reader to generate a list of useful authorities and to appreciate the relevance of those authorities to the grounds of appeal. The argument construction sections concentrate on drafting and refining skeleton arguments, and thinking critically about those arguments through a consideration of potential judicial questions. Our belief is that a student who meaningfully engages with this process should have every chance to deliver a successful moot performance.

It is important to note that each chapter is not the same. Our aim is to underscore that there is no single right way to prepare for a moot; we simply intend to provide guidance and ideas for ways to go about these key tasks. The final chapter provides advice for preparing for advocacy, which is built on our own experiences of the key concerns that students have. It should always be borne in mind, however, that advocacy is a practical skill and to that end any text on the subject will be limited.

Preparing to Moot was not built solely out of our own experiences and efforts. Many of the materials were generated by two of our previous students, Anna Hajilari and Ali Kazi. Anna and Ali undertook preparation for four out of the five moot problem questions and their materials allowed us to build this book. We offer each of them our special thanks for their time, effort and willingness to lay bare their own experiences. We would also like to thank Farukh Bhatti, who spent time capturing Ali and Anna's reflections to help us understand the thought processes behind their preparation. Notably, their work was supported by a small student academic partnership grant from the university, for which we all extend our thanks.

While Ali, Anna and Farukh played a direct role in the development of *Preparing to Moot*, there is no doubt that almost every student we have come across in the context of mooting has contributed in some way, shape or form. Their ideas, successes and blunders have hopefully helped us to better understand the student perspective. Our thanks are also, therefore, extended to all of those students who include, but are not limited to, Jack W, Jade, Chanae, Ellis, Josh, David, James S, Mitica, Uzma, Emma, Anne-Marie, Sarah, Susan, Oliver, Jack R, Mercedes, Dominique, James O and Nathan.

We would also like to thank our colleagues, in particular, Dr Haydn Davies, Professor Maxine Lintern, Lynn Fulford, Jill Molloy, Lauren Haddock, Mark Eccleston-Turner, Rohzeena Janjua and Professor Sue Rivers. All of these individuals have either helped us logistically or acted as valued sounding boards. Particular thanks go to Dr Christy Shucksmith, who drafted and provided guidance to us on the Equity moot problem question. Our thanks also go to all staff at Taylor and Francis who have helped us to shape this project.

Finally, to all those students who are preparing to moot, we hope this book makes the experience a little less mysterious and a lot more enjoyable.

Dr Sarah L. Cooper and Dr Scarlett McArdle
September 2016

TABLE OF LEGAL AUTHORITIES

SCHOLARSHIP

Christian Witting, *Street on Torts*, (14th Edition, Oxford University
Press, 2015). 61
Cohabitation: The Financial Consequences of Relationship Breakdown,
Law Com No. 307 ....157, 161, 168
Donal Nolan, 'Horrifying events and their consequences: clarifying the
operation of the Alcock criteria', (2014) 30(3) *PN* 176. ....62, 63, 71,
77, 78, 83, 180
Janet O'Sullivan and Jonathan Hilliard, *The Law of Contract*
(6th Edition, Oxford University Press, 2014)...130
Kenneth J. Arenson, 'The paradox of disallowing duress as a defence to
murder', (2014) *JCrimL* 65...17, 18, 27
Kirsty Horsey & Erika Rackley, *Tort Law*, (4th Edition, Oxford
University Press, 2015) 61
Liability for Psychiatric Illness, Law Com No 249 (1998) 84, 179
Murder, manslaughter and infanticide,
Law Com No. 304 ....18, 26, 31, 40, 180
Pinar Akman, The relationship between economic duress and abuse of a
dominant position, (2014) 1 *LMCLQ* 132, 137
Richard Hooley, 'Controlling contractual direction', (2013) 72(1)
CLJ 65. ....132, 137, 180
Sharing Homes: A Discussion Paper, Law Com No. 278 ....157, 164, 170

TABLE OF STATUTES

Convention for the Protection of Human Rights and Fundamental
Freedoms, 213 UNTS 222 ....92, 93, 94, 95, 100, 101,
110, 113, 115, 117, 119
Criminal Attempts Act 1981 ....12, 13, 15, 16, 20, 30,
31, 36, 38, 42, 71, 179

Human Rights Act 1998 .... 91, 92, 93, 98, 99, 100, 101,
112, 114, 116–17, 119, 179

TABLE OF CASES

Alcock v Chief Constable of South Yorkshire [1992]
1 AC 310 .... 47, 49, 51, 52, 53, 54, 56,
59, 60, 61, 62, 63, 65, 66, 68,
70, 71, 73, 74, 75, 76, 77, 78,
79, 80, 81, 82, 83, 84, 180
Attorney General's Reference (No.1 of 1992), [1993]
1 WLR 274 .... 16, 22, 31, 38, 39, 42, 178
Barrett v Enfield LBC [2001] 2 AC 550 60
Campbell v Mirror Group Newspapers Ltd [2004]
UKHL 22 .... 86, 96, 97, 98, 100, 103, 106, 108,
110, 111, 113, 114, 115, 118
Cross v Highlands & Islands Enterprise [2001] SLT 1060 60
CTN Cash and Carry Ltd v Gallaher Ltd [1994]
4 All ER 714 .... 123, 124, 128–9, 130, 131,
135, 139, 142, 144
Currie and others v Misa (1874–75) LR 10 Ex. 153 128
Douglas v Hello! Ltd (No.1) [2001]
2 All ER 289 .... 86, 87, 96, 97, 98, 100, 102,
110, 111, 113, 118, 179
Ferdinand v MGN Ltd [2011] EWHC 2454 (QB) 115, 119
Galli-Atkinson v Seghal [2003] EWCA
Civ. 697 .... 59, 63, 67, 68, 80, 83
Holdich v Lothian Health Board [2013] CSOH 197 59
Jones v Kernott [2011] UKSC 53 .... 148, 149, 150, 152, 155, 156,
157, 158, 167, 169, 171
Krone Verlag GmbH & Co KG v Austria [2003]
36 EHRR 57 .... 112, 119
Lloyds Bank Plc v Rosset [1991] AC 107 .... 148, 157, 161, 167
McFarlane v EE Caledonia Ltd [1994] 2 All ER 1. .... 60, 62, 66, 73, 74, 75,
77, 78, 80, 82, 83
McLoughlin v O'Brian [1983] 1 AC 410 .... 61, 62, 63, 64
Midland Bank Plc v Cooke [1995] 4 All ER 562 .... 157, 163, 167
Monk v PC Harrington Ltd [2008] EWHC 1879 59
Mosley v UK, Appl No 48009/08 [2012] EMLR 1 .... 112, 119
Murray v Express Newspapers Plc [2008]
EWCA Civ 446 .... 100, 104, 106, 110, 114, 118

North Ocean Shipping Co v Hyundai Constructors Co
(The Atlantic Baron) [1979] QB 705 ....132, 136, 142
Occidental Worldwide Investment Corporation v Skibs A/S
Avanti (The Sibeon and The Sibotre) [1976]
1 Lloyd's Rep. 293..132, 136, 139, 144
Oxley v Hiscock [2005] Fam 211 ....157, 163, 167, 169
Pao On v Lau Yiu Long [1979] 3 All ER 65 ....132, 135, 139, 141, 142
Paragon Finance Plc v DB Thakerar & Co [1999]
1 All ER 400. ....157, 160
R v Gotts (Benjamin) [1992]
2 AC 412......................................18, 23, 24–5, 31, 35, 36, 39, 40
R v Graham (Paul Anthony) [1982]
1 WLR 294..17, 23, 31, 35, 36, 40
R v Hasan (Aytach), [2005] UKHL 22 ...12, 13, 17, 18, 25–26, 31, 39, 40, 42
R v Howe (Michael Anthony) [1987] 2 WLR 568...............17, 18, 23, 24, 25,
31, 35, 36, 39, 40
R v Ilyas (Mohammed) [1984] 78 Cr App R 17......................16, 21, 31, 39
R v Jones (Kenneth Henry) [1990] 1 WLR 1057............................16, 20, 178
Shorter v Surrey and Sussex Healthcare NHS Trust [2015]
EWHC 614 QB. 60, 69–70, 74, 75, 80, 82
Stack v Dowden [2007] UKHL 17 ....148, 157, 162, 167, 169
Stilk v Myrick [1809] 2 Camp 317 ....132, 133–4, 140, 141, 143
Taylor v A Novo (UK) Ltd [2013] EWCA Civ. 194....................62, 63, 68, 80
Trimingham v Associated Newspapers Ltd [2012]
EWHC 1296 QB 100, 105–6, 108, 113, 119
Von Hannover v Germany, Appl No 40660/08 and
60641/08 [2012] 55 EHRR 15..............................100, 107, 108, 110, 111,
112, 114, 118, 179
Ward v Byham [1956] 1 WLR 496 ....132, 134, 138, 140–1
Westdeutsche Landesbank Girozentrale v Islington London BC
[1996] AC 669 ....157, 159
White v Chief Constable for South Yorkshire [1998] 3 WLR 1509 61
White v Lidl UK GmbH [2005] EWHC 871 (QB).....................................59
Williams v Roffey Bros and Nicholls (Contractors) Ltd [1991]
1 QB 1 ....123, 124, 125, 127, 128, 129, 130, 131,
132, 133, 134, 138, 140, 141, 143
Young v Bristol Aeroplane Co Ltd [1944] KB 7...47

1 CRIMINAL LAW

INTRODUCTION

In this chapter, we show you how to analyse, research and construct an argument in relation to the moot problem presented by the fictitious case of **R v Harper**. This is a criminal law themed moot problem question.

We begin by deconstructing the problem question and introducing you to its basic, but fundamental, features. Next, we focus on summarising the problem question, and consider how you should interpret the grounds of appeal. We then examine how to derive search terms from a problem question in order to allow you to progress on to researching the relevant area of law. Following that, we suggest some preliminary considerations for researchers and show you how to summarise authorities. Finally, we guide you on how to construct legal arguments by providing various example skeleton arguments.

In this question, Ali undertook the roles of Senior Appellant and Senior Respondent, and Anna prepared for the roles of Junior Appellant and Junior Respondent.

ANALYSIS

THE PROBLEM QUESTION

(A) IN THE SUPREME COURT OF THE UNITED KINGDOM

HARPER (B)

V

REGINA (C)

Laura Harper and her two work colleagues, Kate and John, went out in Birmingham to celebrate John's promotion at work. Laura was pleased for John, although she had also applied unsuccessfully for the same position. The three colleagues worked for an international importing company.

At around 11.00pm, the group got into a taxi and requested to go home. Instead, the driver of the taxi locked the doors and took the group to a wooded **(D)** area where a gang of three men were waiting. Kate, John and Laura were stripped of their valuables and beaten. John was also stabbed in the leg with a penknife. The gang repeatedly told Laura, Kate and John they were going to kill them.

The gang tied John to a tree, and told Laura to shoot him. Laura initially refused, but after being threatened with the penknife, she reluctantly held out her hand. The gang member placed a loaded pistol into Laura's hand.

Laura raised the gun, but before putting her finger on the trigger and aiming it, she shouted: '*You are all vile cowards. You haven't got the stomach to finish what you started, so you need me to do it for you! But, John's pain is on your shoulders, not mine.*' However, before she placed her finger on the trigger a team of police swarmed the area and arrested everyone present.

The gang members were all charged and convicted of various offences. **(E)** John and Kate were released with apologies, but Laura was charged with attempted murder.

At the trial, Judge Warren directed the jury that Laura was guilty of **(F)** attempted murder, provided that they were satisfied that when she took the gun and prepared to aim it, she intended to kill John. He directed them further that duress was no defence.

The jury returned a unanimous verdict of guilty. In the circumstances, Judge Warren decided to give Laura an unconditional discharge.

Laura's appeal was dismissed in the Court of Appeal. She now appeals, **(G)** with leave, to the Supreme Court on the grounds that the trial judge misdirected the jury:

H 1. In directing them that an act constituting attempted murder had been committed.

I 2. In his direction that duress was no defence to attempted murder.

UNDERSTANDING THE BASICS OF THE PROBLEM QUESTION

Before you begin to analyse a moot problem question, you should familiarise yourself with its various features. Below you will find a list of features identified by the relevant letter in the problem above. These features will remain loosely the same in most moot problems. The most notable differences occur between civil and criminal law moot problems.

A COURT

The court that you are advocating in dictates a number of things. For example it indicates the significance of precedent. **R v Harper** is in the UK Supreme Court, which is not bound by its own precedent. When advocating in the Supreme Court, it is also worth noting the types of cases that will gain permission to appeal. Cases accepted for argument in the Supreme Court will often be cases of the 'greatest public and constitutional importance'. This fact may influence the type of argument you may seek to make.

B APPELLANT

The first name indicates who is appealing to the appeal court. In **R v Harper**, the defendant (as indicated by the surname of the defendant, i.e. Harper) is appealing the points of law to the Supreme Court.

C RESPONDENT

The second name indicates who is responding to the appeal. In **R v Harper**, the Crown (as indicated by the term 'R' for 'Regina') is responding to the appeal.

D INCIDENT FACTS

The first four paragraphs set out the factual circumstances of the incident that led to the legal issues presented.

E CHARGES

The fifth paragraph sets out the charges levelled against the defendant. In **R v Harper**, the defendant was charged with attempted murder. Remember, 'charges' are typically unique to criminal law problem questions. If the question does not indicate what specific source of law (such as case law or statutory law) defines the crime charged, you should research this as a starting point. This will become more apparent when we begin to identify research terms.

3

F **LONG PROCEDURAL HISTORY**

This explains what has happened in the case in the previous courts where it has been heard. This helps you to understand how and why the current appeal came about.

G **IMMEDIATE PROCEDURAL HISTORY**

This passage tells you what has happened in the court directly below the court in which the moot problem question is in. For example, in **R v Harper** the case was last heard in the Court of Appeal (Criminal Division).

H **GROUND ONE OF THE APPEAL**

This ground 'belongs' to Senior Counsel for both the Appellant and the Respondent, which in this case is Ali. The Appellant will argue for the appeal (i.e. for it to be allowed), whereas the Respondent will argue against (i.e. for it to be dismissed). In **R v Harper**, the Senior Appellant will argue that the trial judge *did* misdirect the jury in saying that an act had been committed that constituted attempted murder, and the Senior Respondent will argue there *was no* error and attempted murder is made out.

I **GROUND TWO OF THE APPEAL**

This ground 'belongs' to Junior Counsel for both the Appellant and the Respondent, which in this case is Anna. Again, the Appellant will argue for the appeal, whereas the Respondent will argue against. In **R v Harper**, the Junior Appellant will argue that the trial judge *did* misdirect the jury in saying that the defence of duress was not applicable to a case of attempted murder, and the Junior Respondent will argue there *was no* error and duress is not applicable.

SUMMARISING THE CASE

When you are familiar with the fundamental features of the moot question, it is useful to construct a summary of the fact pattern that includes all of the salient points. This will help ensure that you know the facts thoroughly, but also it is routine for judges to request a brief summary of the problem question.

This section first reviews the summaries constructed by Ali and Anna. These are used as a springboard to show you some of the difficulties mooters can have when constructing summaries that are both concise and comprehensive. It is important to note that there is no magic formula for creating a summary; however, we employ the following general 'rule of thumb' and encourage students to develop summaries that comprise five key points (plus the grounds of appeal) and articulated in clear, simple and professional language (i.e. largely absent the use of legalese).

Below is the summary constructed by Ali:

* *Three work colleagues, Laura, John and Kate, were out in Birmingham city centre.*
* *At 11.00pm they called a taxi and asked the driver to take them home; instead he drove them to a wooded area where a gang of men were waiting.*
* *The gang took their valuables, beat them and repeatedly told them they would kill them. John was stabbed in the leg with a penknife.*
* *John was tied to a tree and Laura was told to shoot him. She refused at first but reluctantly agreed after further threats were made.*
* *A loaded pistol was placed in Laura's hand. She shouted, 'You are all vile cowards. You haven't got the stomach to finish what you started, so need me to do it for you! But, John's pain is on your shoulders, not mine.'*
* *She raised the gun but before she could put her finger on the trigger the police arrived and arrested all parties.*
* *Laura was charged and convicted of attempted murder. The judge directed the jury that she was guilty if they were satisfied that she had the intention to kill when she prepared to aim the gun. He also directed them that duress was no defence.*
* *Laura's appeal was dismissed in the Court of Appeal.*
* *She appeals to the Supreme Court on the grounds that the judge misdirected the jury in directing them that an act constituting attempted murder had been committed, and that duress was no defence to attempted murder.*

Ali clearly focused on constructing a summary that did not neglect important facts. The result is quite a detailed summary. While this is a good approach to start with, the summary above is perhaps a little too detailed and would have benefitted from further editing. In its current form, it includes too many extraneous details, and would take too long to deliver to the judge. Ali's decision to use bullet points, however, is a useful one. It gives his synopsis both structure and clarity, particularly with regards to the chronology of events. All of these things are helpful when advocating.

Below is the summary constructed by Anna:

Laura, Kate and John went out to celebrate John's promotion. When they got in the taxi the driver took them to another area. A gang took their belongings and beat them up. Laura was told to shoot John and was handed a loaded gun. Before putting her finger on the trigger the police showed up. Laura is now accused of committing the offence of attempted murder.

Anna's summary is significantly different to Ali's. First, she summarises in prose as opposed to bullet points. Second, she has attempted to rephrase the language of the question to enable her to be concise. Third, her summary is vastly less detailed than Ali's. While Ali's concern was to not miss out detail, Anna was more focused on providing a short, sharp summary that would be presentable to a judge in a concise and speedy manner. This is an important aspect of a summary; however, overall Anna's summary needs further development. Anna's approach currently lacks important facts and is not fully accurate. For example, her summary ends with Laura Harper being *accused* of attempted murder, whereas the moot problem is staged way beyond that point, as [by now] Harper has been convicted of attempted murder, has appealed that conviction and is now appealing to the Supreme Court.

Below is an example of a summary we developed to try and take a middle ground between Ali's desire to be comprehensive and Anna's desire to be concise.

- *The Appellant and her friends were kidnapped, robbed and beaten by a gang. The Appellant was ordered to shoot one of her friends by a member of the gang. The Appellant refused but after being threatened with a weapon, she reluctantly held out her hand and a loaded pistol was placed in it.*
- *The Appellant raised the gun but did not put her finger on the trigger and stated that any suffering to her friend would be the gang's responsibility. At that point, police intervened.*
- *The Appellant was charged with attempted murder.*
- *At trial, the judge directed the jury that if they were satisfied that when the Appellant took the gun and aimed it, she intended to kill her friend, then she would be guilty of attempted murder and, second, that duress is no defence. The Appellant was convicted.*
- *The Appellant appealed that both of those directions were erroneous. This was dismissed by the Court of Appeal. The Appellant now makes the same arguments to the Supreme Court.*

In developing the above summary, we started by condensing the incident. Notice that, in doing so, we rephrased the language of the problem question to allow us to be succinct, yet comprehensive. This is shown by, for example, the fact that our first sentence sets out information that Ali covers in four of his bullet points, namely that the group were kidnapped, robbed and beaten by a gang. Rephrasing the language of a problem question in order to produce a summary is perfectly acceptable – just be sure not to change the meaning of the content when doing so.

In our summary, we have highlighted facts that are pertinent to the particular grounds of appeal and left out others that are peripheral. With regards to the first ground of appeal, which focuses on the charge of attempted murder, it was important for us to include facts that would be relevant to the Appellant's physical actions and state of mind. This meant, for example, that particularly relevant facts included the Appellant being beaten and threatened, and that she was reluctant to take the gun and orally abdicated responsibility for any resulting harm. The point at which the police intervened is also important. It is much less important to consider facts like where the incident took place, what time of day it was, how the group were travelling and what was taken from them. These were some of the mistakes Ali and Anna made. These peripheral facts do not have any material impact on the creation of a summary.

With regards to the second ground of appeal, which focuses on the defence of duress, it was important for us to include facts that were relevant to the 'pressure' the Appellant was put under at the time of the incident. This meant, for example, that facts related to the Appellant being beaten and threatened with a weapon were also relevant for the second ground of appeal.

Second, in a criminal law themed question you should always include the charge, conviction and findings of the lower courts. There is no need to go into a lot of detail on the charge; it simply needs to be stated. The findings of the lower courts are especially relevant in the case of **R v Harper** because what happened in the trial court (specifically the directions given by the trial judge) is what has generated the current grounds of appeal before the Supreme Court. This is why the exact directions of the judge should be included in the summary. An appropriate way to end a summary is with the exact issues that are before the court. This gives the judge a clear journey from the original incident (that generated the criminal liability) right up to the appeal being argued.

UNDERSTANDING YOUR GROUND OF APPEAL

The next thing you need to consider is the precise argument that you need to make. This will be specified in the grounds of appeal. A mooter (like a lawyer!) can only argue the grounds that have been certified (i.e. allowed) before the court. Each mooter has an accepted ground and angle that they should be arguing. If a mooter strays away from their ground, then it is perfectly acceptable for a judge to refuse to hear their arguments.

In **R v Harper**, the first ground of appeal argues that the trial judge erred in his direction that an act amounting to attempted murder had been committed by Harper. The Senior Appellant, therefore, could not make an argument that focused on another criminal offence, such as murder or possession of an offensive weapon. The Senior Respondent would be restricted in the same way. Ground two of the appeal argues that the trial judge erred in his direction that duress was no defence to attempted murder. The Junior Appellant, therefore, must focus on arguing that duress applies to the offence of attempted murder only, and not focus on duress applying to other crimes (although, of course, the mooter can use the application of duress to other crimes as a method of persuading the judge to apply the defence to attempted murder). Again, the Junior Respondent would be restricted in the same way.

You must clearly understand the point of your ground of appeal. A good way to do this is by asking yourself simple questions, such as, in the context of **R v Harper**:

- Am I arguing for the appeal to be allowed or dismissed?
- Am I arguing that Harper committed or did not commit attempted murder?
- Am I arguing that duress does or does not apply to an offence of attempted murder?
- Am I saying that the trial judge erred or was correct in his direction?

These questions can act as your safety net. If you always grasp the basics of the point that you are arguing, then you will always have a central idea to keep coming back to. This will help you should you encounter tough questioning; it will assist you not to concede your ground of appeal. These sorts of questions are also useful when it comes to argument construction, especially when deciding how to use sources of law, such as whether you want the court to distinguish or overrule a common law precedent. At this initial stage, however, they act as a point of clarification for your own understanding.

Below we answer these questions for each mooter in **R v Harper** to give you an idea of how they help.

	Senior Appellant	Junior Appellant	Senior Respondent	Junior Respondent
Am I arguing for the appeal to be allowed or dismissed?	Allowed	Allowed	Dismissed	Dismissed
Am I arguing that Harper committed or did not commit attempted murder?	Did not commit	N/A	Did commit	N/A
Am I arguing that duress does or does not apply to an offence of attempted murder?	N/A	Does apply	N/A	Does not apply
Am I saying that the trial judge erred or was correct in his direction?	Erred (direction one)	Erred (direction two)	Did not err (direction one)	Did not err (direction two)

SELECTING YOUR RESEARCH TERMS

This section helps you move from analysing the problem question to beginning your research. The task of research can be daunting so it is important that you remain focused. In order to do this, we asked Ali and Anna to take a systematic approach to selecting their research terms, focusing on the first five paragraphs of the moot problem. We asked each of them to, per paragraph, select two types of research terms: obvious terms or words from the question (that do not have to be strictly word-for-word) and then hidden terms that they might derive from their existing legal knowledge, as well as any relevant synonyms.

Ali continued preparing for the roles of Senior Appellant and Respondent. Naturally, these two roles will be looking for the same terms; they will simply diverge when it comes to constructing an argument.

Below is Ali's attempt for the Senior Appellant and Respondent:

Paragraph	Obvious Research Terms	Hidden Research Terms
1		
2		causation
3	loaded pistol, initially refused, held out her hand, reluctantly	pistol, gun, firearm, weapon
4	raised the gun. before she placed her finger on the trigger, police, arrested everyone	prepare, preparatory, interrupted, prevented, *actus reus*
5	attempted murder, intended to kill, took the gun, prepared to aim	attempt, try, *actus reus*, *mens rea*, intent, intention, direct intent, indirect intent, oblique intent, more than merely preparatory

When Ali was choosing his terms, he was already aware of the landscape of criminal law. As such, he was keen to focus on phrases possibly associated with *actus reus* and *mens rea*, which are the building blocks for most crimes. Ali begins from the point that, as a crime that doesn't involve strict liability, attempted murder is made up of these two elements and both should be considered. This is an intelligent approach to take and makes good use of his existing knowledge. Remember there is nothing wrong with using what you know already! Ali also shows an appreciation that synonyms are useful in the research process, as they offer the researcher options for researching the same idea in different ways.

Anna continued preparing for the roles of Junior Appellant and Respondent. Again, naturally, these roles will both consider the same terms and focus on the same area at this point in the process. Below is Anna's attempt for the Junior Appellant and Respondent:

Paragraph	Obvious Research Terms	Hidden Research Terms
1	pleased, applied unsuccessfully	
2	got into taxi, requested to go home, locked the doors, wooded area, gang of three, stripped of their valuables, beaten, stabbed in the leg, penknife, repeatedly, going to kill them	unlawful imprisonment, battery, actual bodily harm (ABH), grievous bodily harm (GBH), sharp weapon, assault

3	tied John to a tree, shoot him, initially refused, threatened, reluctantly, placed a loaded pistol into Laura's hand	hesitant, no intention, no preparatory acts
4	raised the gun, before putting her finger on the trigger, John's pain, before she placed her finger	
5	attempted murder	

Anna focused initially on factual points that would help build up an idea of a threat to the Appellant. This was a good starting point for a ground of appeal concerning duress. She does, however, include a number of terms that would not necessarily be relevant to the concept of duress. In her zeal to include terms from across the question, she has made the common mistake of crossing over into the other ground of appeal, as some of the terms she has selected would, in fact, solely assist with researching ground one of the appeal. If you consider, in particular, the terms listed in paragraph four, these are not necessarily relevant for her discussion of duress. Moreover, she does not include the term 'duress' anywhere in her terms, which, although not stated in paragraphs one to five, is a term that should have been evident from the grounds of appeal and preliminary reading. Anna may have neglected to include the term 'duress' because, understandably, it is so obvious. However, when preparing to research it is best to be thorough, which includes stating the obvious.

Not every paragraph of the question will yield something relevant to both grounds of appeal. Picking too many search terms is a classic mistake and an easy one to make. It is important to keep a focus on your overarching point. A way to keep your selection focused is by undertaking some basic reading beforehand. Reviewing relevant chapter(s) in a standard undergraduate text-book is an easy way to do this. Once you have read around the area, you should be better able to judge what is and is not relevant, research wise.

After completing such reading, we generated the following research terms for both grounds of appeal.

Ground One

Paragraph	Obvious Research Terms	Hidden Research Terms
1		
2	beaten, threat to kill	kidnapped, robbed, injured, threatened
3	ordered to shoot, refused, threatened with a weapon, loaded pistol	ordered, directed, told, unwilling, loaded weapon/gun/firearm, motive, aim and purpose, virtually certain, victim secured/unable to move
4	finger, trigger, raised	verbal, intervened, aim/aimed prepared, refused/declined responsibility
5	attempted murder	Criminal Attempts Act 1981

In addition to the above terms, the procedural history and grounds of appeal give rise to additional legal terms that will be relevant to your research, such as, for example, 'attempted murder'. The judge's direction, in forming the core of the grounds of appeal, should also be borne in mind when examining the particular area of law.

Ground Two

Paragraph	Obvious Research Terms	Hidden Research Terms
1		
2	wooded area, gang of three, robbed, beaten, stabbed, penknife, repeated threats to kill	weapon, injury, wounded, kidnapped, secluded area, harmed, threat of death, immediate
3	told to shoot, threatened with a penknife, reluctantly	ordered to shoot
4	pain	pressurised, no other option, threats, duress of threats
5		R v Hasan (Aytach) [2005] UKHL 22

Again, the procedural history of the case and the grounds of appeal will give rise to additional terms. Here, for example, the ground is explicit in considering whether duress can be a defence to attempted murder. This would require an understanding of duress and the law surrounding its application, or not, in cases of attempted murder.

The main difference between our attempt and those of the students is that it includes fewer terms from the actual problem question, i.e. obvious terms, and focuses more on hidden legal terminology and alternative phrasing. Obviously, this is only possible after some initial reading around the topic and demonstrates the importance of getting a basic grasp on the area before generating research terms. For example, in ground one, we include the Criminal Attempts Act 1981, which is the seminal statute governing the crime of attempt. In addition, we derive the word 'aim', as this is a natural way to describe someone's handling of a gun. With regards to ground two, we include the phrase 'duress of threats' because we know that this is distinct from the defence of 'duress of circumstance' and **R v Harper** is an example of the former. In addition to this, we use the phrase 'ordered to shoot', as this is another conventional way to describe someone being told to do something. We also include a seminal case – *R v Hasan* – which our pre-reading highlighted to us as important to the area of law.

SUMMARY

This section has shown you how to analyse a criminal law moot problem question. We have done this by highlighting the problem question's fundamental features, and considering ways to summarise the problem question, interpret the grounds of appeal and generate initial research terms. We will utilise these research terms in the next section, which focuses on undertaking legal research for **R v Harper**.

RESEARCH

This section focuses on how to research the areas of law relevant to **R v Harper**. This problem question is almost entirely common law-centric in that the grounds of appeal lend themselves to a consideration of related case law. As you will see, the grounds of appeal require the mooter to develop a clear knowledge of the case law and how it will be approached by the Appellant and Respondent. As such, this section concentrates on developing your research skills in identifying, interpreting and applying the common law.

PRELIMINARY CONSIDERATIONS FOR RESEARCHERS

Before starting to research your ground of appeal, always be clear on the following things:

- **The rules.** All competitions will have strict rules and these will include rules on how many authorities each mooting team or mooter is able to use. Often, the competition rules will dictate the number of different types of sources – for example, how many cases you are able to use.
- **Read.** Make sure that you have done some initial reading in the area. You will find your research quite difficult and, in particular, unfocused, without doing this.
- **Know where to start.** Your initial reading should direct you on where is a good place to start. For instance, it should highlight to you key pieces of legislation or key cases that need to be considered.
- **Know where to look.** Be sure to use appropriate and authoritative legal sources. This includes paper resources in the library but for most law students this will primarily mean valid legal databases, such as LexisNexis, Westlaw, BAIILI and JustCite. We also encourage students to 'find their feet' in the topic area by reading an introductory textbook. This can provide an excellent introduction and foundation, but be aware that such sources cannot be used as authority within a moot.
- **Avoid easy shortcuts.** While it may be very easy to look on internet search engines, such as Google, this can often lead to students using inaccurate and/or inappropriate sources. Using the internet is fine, but you need to appreciate what sources you are considering and whether they are worth giving any value to.
- **Keep track.** You need to make sure that you keep a full research trail throughout your research process. Keep a pen and paper to hand and track every step that you make. This is so you can retrace your steps.

RESEARCHING R V HARPER

The rules in relation to **R v Harper** allowed Ali and Anna to each use three cases, any relevant legislation and two 'other' sources, such as journal articles and Law Commission reports.

Before beginning their research, we asked both students to categorise the search terms that they had developed at the end of their analysis of the moot problem. The students were also asked to explain their rationale behind choosing such terms and categories. We then asked them to undertake research and generate a list of chosen authorities. Below we consider ground one and ground two in turn.

Ground One

These are the categories and terms selected by Ali:

Categories	Terms
Actus reus	'held out' w/s hand, raised w/s gun, aim! w/s gun, finger w/s trigger, preparatory, 'more than merely preparatory'
Mens rea	'direct intent', 'indirect intent', 'intention', 'intention to kill', 'intended to kill', reluctan!
Crucial terms	attempted murder, *actus reus*, *mens rea*, Criminal Attempts Act 1981
Minor terms	interrupt, prevent!, interfere!, causation, 'factual causation', 'but for', aggravating factors, mitigating factors, duress, compulsion, coercion, force, pressure

Ali focused on the requirements of the relevant criminal law concept, i.e. attempted murder. Ali realised from his initial reading that his ground of appeal would come down to a consideration of whether or not the *actus reus* and *mens rea* required for an offence of attempted murder were present or not. He therefore clearly allocated a category of terms to each of these elements. His final two categories included terms that he considered to be significantly relevant and peripheral, respectively.

It is also interesting that Ali has also already begun developing his search terms into appropriate forms for undertaking research using online databases. For instance, he uses terms and connectors such as 'w/s' and truncators such as the '!' symbol. Using these devices (as appropriate to the relevant database) will have allowed Ali to conduct more efficient and focused research. This is due to such phrasing retrieving more results and often leading to more precise research.

A knowledge of how to use such terms, connectors and truncators can be invaluable when using online legal databases. You should be aware that there are a wide range of such research tools and that there can be a slight differentiation between databases in how they apply. However, most online databases tend to provide guides on what their database uses and how. Below we summarise how these tools could have helped Ali in his research:

- **'Held out' w/s hand** – using this combination of terms and connectors would have retrieved sources that included the word 'hand' in the same sentence as the phrase 'held out'.
- **Raised w/s gun** – using this combination of terms and connectors would have retrieved sources that included the word 'gun' in the same sentence as the word 'raised'.
- **'factual causation'** – using quotation marks around a phrase will have retrieved sources that included that phrase.
- **Aim!** – using this truncator would have retrieved sources including variations of the word 'aim', such as 'aiming' and 'aimed'.
- **Reluctan!** – using this truncator would have retrieved sources including variations of words starting with 'Reluctan' such as 'reluctant', 'reluctance' and 'reluctantly'.

In using these sort of terms and connectors, Ali generated the following sources:

- **Criminal Attempts Act 1981 s1 (1).**
- *R v Jones* **(Kenneth Henry) [1990] 1 WLR 1057.**
- *R v Ilyas* **(Mohammed) [1984] 78 Cr App R 17.**
- **Attorney General's Reference (No. 1 of 1992), [1993] 1 WLR 274.**

Ground Two

These are the categories and terms selected by Anna:

Category	Research Terms
Intention/revenge	applied unsuccessfully, pleased, possible revenge
Immediate threats	unlawful imprisonment, battery, ABH, GBH, sharp item, assault, threats, beaten, stabbed, gang of three, penknife, going to kill them
Threat of death	tied John, shoot him, refused, threatened, reluctantly, no intention, no preparatory acts
Crime	attempted murder

Anna's rationale for choosing these categories and terms was to reflect the requirements for the general defence of duress by threats as relevant to the **R v Harper** case. The requirements of duress by threats became evident to Anna through her initial reading.

Anna showed a different approach in researching using her selected research terms. Her research trail shows this:

Begin with Journals.

Step One: Log-on to Westlaw UK and conduct a free text search of the journals using the terms 'duress of threats'.
This produced 314 results.

Step Two: Narrow the results by subject area, i.e. those relevant to criminal law.
This narrowed my list to 67 results.

Step Three: Narrow the results to relevant crime, using the phrase 'attempted murder'.
This produced the following article that was relevant to both attempted murder and the defence of duress:

> ***The paradox of disallowing duress as a defence to murder.* JCrimL 2014, 78 (1), 65–79.**

After searching journal articles, then focus upon case law.

Step One: Search within the cases section of Westlaw UK. Use the term 'attempted murder' within the free text option.
This produced 651 results.

Step Two: Narrow results by subject area, i.e. restrict results to those cases concerned with 'duress' and then further narrow by those duress cases concerned with 'multiple threats'. This produced 13 cases. I began with the first cases returned by the search. These cases were:

> ***R v Howe (Michael Anthony)* [1987] 2 WLR 568.**
> ***R v Graham (Paul Anthony)* [1982] 1 WLR 294.**
> ***R v Hasan (Aytach)* [2005] UKHL 22.**

Step Three: Log on to LexisNexis UK and repeat the same process in terms of searching and narrowing for case law. If the same cases come up then you can be confident in your research. If different cases arise, then retrace your steps and try to consider whether you have made any errors at any point.

Anna provides a systematic yet relatively 'anecdotal' research trail, which is instructive for someone beginning to undertake research. It provides an insight into Anna's thought process during the course of her research. Anna shows that when utilising legal databases, it can be useful to do a general search in relevant source categories (such as journal articles and case law) that will produce a wide set of results, which the researcher can then narrow using terms that are more particular to the case they are dealing with, and, thus, more likely to generate relevant and useful sources to construct an argument. Anna's last statement with regard to the use of LexisNexis UK demonstrates that she is trying to conduct comprehensive research. Evidently, Anna utilises Westlaw UK as her main database for research and then uses LexisNexis UK as a verification 'tool' to check her work and ensure that the same sources are coming up. In light of this research, Anna produced the following list of sources:

- *R v Graham* (Paul Anthony) [1982] 1 WLR 294.

- *R v Howe* (Michael Anthony) [1987] 2 WLR 568.

- *R v Gotts* (Benjamin) [1992] 2 AC 412.

- *R v Hasan* (Aytach) [2005] UKHL 22.

- Murder, manslaughter and infanticide, Law Com No. 304.

- Kenneth J. Arenson, *The paradox of disallowing duress as a defence to murder*, (2014) JCrimL 65.

SUMMARISING THE RELEVANCE OF AUTHORITIES

Once you have selected your authorities, you must summarise their relevance so that you can construct a useful argument.

The below tables summarise the authorities chosen by Ali and Anna in relation to the grounds of appeal. Not only can you use these sorts of tables to guide your argument construction, but they are also useful to have to hand when mooting as they can act as a quick memory refresher.

Ground One

	Criminal Appeals Act 1981 s(1)
Type of Source	Statute/legislation
Full Citation	**Criminal Appeals Act 1981 section 1, sub-section 1**
Persuasiveness	Statute is binding upon the courts in that the courts have no choice but to interpret the language as provided.
Relevance to the Grounds of Appeal	This is a key authority because it defines the crime of attempt and outlines the requisite *mens rea* and *actus reus*.
	The provision reads, '*If, with intent to commit an offence to which this section applies, a person does an act which is more than merely preparatory to the commission of the offence, he is guilty of attempting to commit the offence.*'
	The Appellant will seek to establish that this definition is not satisfied on the instant facts (with reference to relevant law), whereas the Respondent will argue it is.
	It is worth noting that the law of attempts has been reviewed by the Law Commission in the last ten years. The Law Commission's report was published in December 2009, recommending reforms. You can access the report here: www.gov.uk/government/uploads/system/uploads/ attachment_data/file/248029/0041.pdf. The government has not yet acted formally on the Law Commission's recommendations.

R v Jones

Type of Source Case law

Full Citation *R v Jones (Kenneth Henry)* [1990] 1 WLR 1057

Persuasiveness This case was heard in the Court of Appeal (Criminal Division). While it may be persuasive, it is not binding upon the Supreme Court.

Relevance to the Grounds of Appeal This case focuses on the *actus reus* of attempt.

The court found that, the words 'more than merely preparatory' in the Criminal Attempts Act 1981 s1(1) do not mean the 'last act within his power'. Jones' appeal that because he still had to perform three further acts to complete the full offence of attempt, namely (1) remove the safety catch of the gun being pointed at the victim; (2) put his finger on the trigger and (3) pull the trigger, was rejected.

The court in *Jones* stated that the words of s1(1) are to be given their 'natural meaning'. In so stating, the court was ruling that a common-sense approach to the interpretation of this law should be taken.

Jones is factually similar to **R v Harper**. The case involved a charge of attempted murder and the handling of a firearm by the defendant. This means that it will likely be considered to be a particularly persuasive authority by the Supreme Court considering Harper's appeal. The Appellant will likely argue that the court should distinguish *Jones*. They could do this by arguing that, on the facts provided, Jones' actions went further than Harper's, and therefore Harper does not meet the requirements of an attempt. The Respondent will likely urge the court to follow *Jones* on the basis that the facts are so similar.

Using the case analysis function on Westlaw UK, it is evident that the findings of the court in this case have been positively applied in subsequent cases. In other words, the courts are agreeing with the approach taken by the Court of Appeal in this case that an attempt does not require the defendant to do the 'last act within his power'.

R v Ilyas (Mohammed)

Type of Source   Case law

Full Citation   *R v Ilyas (Mohammed)* [1984] 78 Cr App R 17

Persuasiveness   This case was heard in the Court of Appeal (Criminal Division). While it may be persuasive, it is not binding upon the Supreme Court.

Relevance to the Grounds of Appeal   This case focuses on the *actus reus* of attempt.

In this case, the Court of Appeal found that where a defendant is charged with an attempt to commit an offence, the case should be withdrawn from the jury if either he has not done every act necessary in order to achieve the intended result, or the acts done are merely preparatory and remote from the contemplated offence.

Mohammed was charged with dishonestly attempting to obtain property by deception. He had falsely reported to the police and his insurance company that his car had been stolen, and he had obtained but not completed a claim form from his insurance company.

The court found that the case should have been withdrawn from the jury. Mohammed had plainly not done every act which was necessary for him to do to achieve the result he intended, i.e. all he had done was to obtain a claim form. Doing that act and all the other acts preceding it were merely preparatory and remote from the contemplated offence of dishonestly attempting to obtain money from the insurance company. He did not go beyond mere preparation.

This case involves a different offence of attempt than that in **R v Harper.** The court, therefore, may think that it is not overly helpful. Still, the Appellant could use *Mohammed* to argue that Harper has not done every act needed to achieve the relevant result. For example, she had not put her finger on the trigger. The Respondent could argue, however, that Harper's preceding acts, such as taking the gun, were not remote from the contemplated offence, and therefore an attempt is satisfied. These types of arguments are a good example of how adversaries can rely on the same case to make an argument in their own favour.

Attorney General Reference No. 1

Type of Source   Case law

Full Citation   Attorney General's Reference (No. 1 of 1992), [1993] 1 WLR 274

Persuasiveness   This case was heard in the Court of Appeal (Criminal Division). While it may be persuasive, it is not binding upon the Supreme Court.

Relevance to the Grounds of Appeal   This was a referred case. This means that the Attorney-General referred the issue brought up by the case (whether, on a charge of attempted rape, it was necessary for the prosecution, as a matter of law, to prove attempted penetration) to the court for resolution.

This case considered the offence of attempted rape. The court held that, for the crime of attempted rape to be raised, it is not necessary for the prosecution to prove that the defendant physically attempted to penetrate with his penis, in order to fulfil the *actus reus* of attempt. Where there is evidence from which the intent to rape can be inferred and acts more than merely preparatory to the commission of the offence were proved, the offence can be made out. The defendant's acts in the case involved him straddling the victim, but he was yet to remove his or her clothes or perform unequivocal sex acts. This was sufficient evidence of attempt to be left to the jury.

This case involves a different offence of attempt than that in **R v Harper**. The court, therefore, may think that it is not overly helpful. The Appellant could use this case to argue that Harper's case did not involve 'sufficient evidence'. Unlike in this case, it is not clear that Harper had an intention to kill, and her acts in handling the gun were not as sufficient as the defendant's action to straddle the victim in the Attorney General's Reference case. As such, the Appellant could argue the judge should not have left open the question of attempt to the jury in Harper's case. The Respondent could argue that Harper's actions to handle the gun and make a statement that suggested her friends would be killed are equal to the straddling of the victim in the Attorney General's Reference Case, and therefore the judge was right to direct the jury as he did.

Ground Two

R v Graham

Type of Source   Case law

Full Citation   *R v Graham (Paul Anthony)* [1982] 1 WLR 294

Persuasiveness   This case was heard in the Court of Appeal (Criminal Division). It will have persuasive effect but will not be binding upon the Supreme Court.

Relevance to the Grounds of Appeal   In this case the defendant had been drinking and taking drugs, and was involved (along with his male partner) in killing his wife. He was tried on a charge of murder, and claimed duress arguing that his anxiety and intake of drugs would have made him more susceptible to threats by his male partner, who was violent.

Lord Chief Justice Lane stated that the correct direction for the jury in cases of duress is:

'*(1) Was the defendant, or may he have been, impelled to act as he did because, as a result of what he reasonably believed King [Graham's partner] had said or done, he had good cause to fear that if he did not so act King would kill him or (if this is to be added) cause him serious physical injury? (2) If so, have the prosecution made the jury sure that a sober person of reasonable firmness, sharing the characteristics of the defendant, would not have responded to whatever he reasonably believed King said or did by taking part in the killing?*'

The court made it clear that the fact that a defendant's will to resist has been eroded by the voluntary consumption of drink or drugs or both is not relevant to this test.

In effect, *Graham* provides the criteria a defendant must satisfy in order to establish duress. As such, the Appellant in **R v Harper** (if they can convince the court duress does apply to attempted murder) will need to argue that Harper satisfies these criteria. The Respondent will need to be prepared to challenge this as an alternative argument, as the most obvious course of action for the Respondent to argue first is that duress does not apply to offences of attempted murder. The cases of *Howe* and *Gotts* summarised below explain why this is the case.

R v Howe and others

Type of Source Case law

Full Citation *R v Howe (Michael Anthony)* [1987] 2 WLR 568

Persuasiveness This is a House of Lords case. The Supreme Court is not bound by the decisions of its predecessor (the House of Lords), but the holdings of this court are very carefully considered.

Relevance to the Grounds of Appeal This is a conjoined appeals case. This is when an appeal court considers multiple (unrelated) cases that raise the same or similar legal questions. It is important to know how the court determined each separate case.

In this case, the House of Lords held that duress cannot be a defence to murder, and, in *obiter dictum* stated that it should also not be available to a charge of attempted murder. The rationale for this was that because attempted murder requires proof of an intent to kill, whereas for an offence of murder it is sufficient to prove an intent to cause really serious injury, it cannot be right to allow the defence to one who may be more intent upon taking a life than the murderer.

Obiter dictum is merely an expression of a judge's opinion, but is not essential to the legal question at hand and therefore not binding as precedent.

Howe is the starting point of the Respondent's argument for ground two of the appeal. This is because it provides the first formal (although not binding) pronouncement by the House of Lords that duress does not apply in cases of attempted murder. The Appellant will, of course, underscore the non-binding nature of this statement.

R v Gotts

Type of Source Case law

Full Citation *R v Gotts (Benjamin)* [1992] 2 AC 412

Persuasiveness This is a House of Lords case. The Supreme Court is not bound by the decisions of its predecessor (the House of Lords), but the holdings of this court are very carefully considered.

Relevance to the Grounds of Appeal	Gotts was ordered by his father to kill his mother otherwise the father would shoot him. Gotts subsequently stabbed his mother causing her serious, but not fatal, injuries. Gotts was charged with attempted murder and the trial judge ruled that the defence of duress was not available to him. He pleaded guilty and then appealed the judge's ruling.

The House of Lords followed the *obiter dicta* statement from *Howe* and held that the defence of duress was not available for attempted murder.

Gotts is central to the Respondent's case. The Respondent will argue that *Gotts* is a long-established precedent and should be followed in **R v Harper**. *Gotts* is a difficult obstacle for the Appellant. One course of action the Appellant could take, however, is to argue that the court would be justified in departing from *Gotts* in narrow circumstances, such as those present in the Harper case, which involve significant violence towards the defendant.

R v Hasan

Type of Source	Case law
Full Citation	*R v Hasan (Aytach)* [2005] UKHL 22
Persuasiveness	This is a House of Lords case. The Supreme Court is not bound by the decisions of its predecessor (the House of Lords), but the holdings of this court are very carefully considered.
Relevance to the Grounds of Appeal	Hasan worked for a woman who ran an escort agency involving prostitution. He would drive women to clients and act as a minder. His employer became involved with a violent drug dealer, X. X took over much of Hasan's work and friction developed between the two. The Appellant was aware that X was a dangerous man. X and another man ambushed Hasan. X told Hasan to commit a burglary on a house and threatened that if he did not do so he and his family would be harmed. Hasan complied and was convicted of aggravated burglary. His defence of duress was rejected by the jury.

The court ruled that the defence of duress was excluded when, as a result of the accused's voluntary association with others engaged in criminal activity, he foresaw or ought reasonably to have foreseen the risk of being subjected to any compulsion by threats of violence.

Lord Bingham stated,

' *The policy of the law must be to discourage association with known criminals, and it should be slow to excuse the criminal conduct of those who do so. If a person voluntarily becomes or remains associated with others engaged in criminal activity in a situation where he knows or ought reasonably to know that he may be the subject of compulsion by them or their associates, he cannot rely on the defence of duress to excuse any act which he is thereafter compelled to do by them.*'

The court further outlined the elements of duress, namely that there must be a specified crime immediate threat, threat of death or serious injury, the threat of violence must be to the defendant or a person for whom he has responsibility, and the threat must be so great as to overbear the ordinary powers of human resistance.

Hasan is the most recent articulation of the boundaries of the defence of duress. Moreover, it affirms that duress is not a defence in cases of attempted murder. As such, the Respondent will likely argue that the court in Harper should continue the precedent set in *Gotts* and affirmed in *Hasan*. The Appellant will need to confront this line of precedent.

Law Commission Report No. 304

Type of Source   Report by an independent body that is statutory obliged to keep the law under review and to recommend reform where it is needed.

Full Citation   Murder, manslaughter and infanticide, Law Com No. 304

Persuasiveness   The Law Commission's comments and recommendations are not binding on the courts, but can be a helpful source when interpreting the law.

Relevance to the Grounds of Appeal	The Law Commission recommended, *inter alia*, that duress should be a full defence to first degree murder, second degree murder and attempted murder.

The Law Commission's report is most helpful to the Appellant in the Harper case. It is a source the Appellant can use to confront the line of precedent that holds duress is not a defence in cases of attempted murder. They can do this by arguing that research that is more recent than any of the relevant case law argues that duress should apply to help the law achieve 'clarity and coherence'.

The Respondent, however, should underscore that Parliament has not acted on the Law Commission's recommendations, and this may well suggest that the Law Commission's recommendations are unlikely to be implemented given the time lapse between publication and the instant time frame. The Respondent could, therefore, urge the court to take the view that they should not interfere and redefine the law, when Parliament has chosen not to.

The Paradox of Disallowing Duress as a Defence to Murder

Type of Source	Journal article
Full Citation	Kenneth J. Arenson, *The paradox of disallowing duress as a defence to murder*, (2014) JCrimL 65.
Persuasiveness	Scholarship is not binding on any court, but, if relevant, may be persuasive and helpful.
Relevance to the Grounds of Appeal	This article recognises that the common law has declined to allow the defence of duress to be interposed in like manner as a partial defence to the crime of murder, and suggests a number of reforms.

This article focuses on the offence of murder, as opposed to attempted murder, and is mainly concerned with the common law approach taken in Australia. The Appellant and Respondent in **R v Harper**, however, may wish to review the scholar's research in order to shape the phrasing of their own arguments.

SUMMARY

There are any number of different approaches that can be taken towards researching an area of law. The aim is always going to be the same; ensure that you have a solid understanding of the relevant area of law and are able to identify the key authorities that will assist you in building a strong argument. Ali and Anna both achieve this aim but through different means. In spite of taking differing approaches, however, both generally seek to achieve the same core pieces of knowledge about their sources. Each student recognises the importance of understanding what type of source they select, what the status of that source is and why it might be used.

Research is a skill that is improved over time. You will be able to learn different techniques and approaches and, hopefully, Ali and Anna's approaches have shown you some new ideas to try in developing your skills. These are skills that will improve with practice.

Research can also be a task that seems never ending; there will always be another piece of academic opinion or another case to consider. It is just as important to know when to stop as it is to know where to start. If you reach a point in your research where you feel confident that you know the key authorities in the area, then you are ready to move on to constructing your argument. Remember, research may be a process that you return to during the course of preparing for a moot. Once you understand the area of law and its relevance for your argument, however, you are ready to begin the next part of your preparation: constructing your argument.

ARGUMENT CONSTRUCTION

In Ali and Anna's work on **R v Harper** so far, any consideration that they have made of authorities has been largely neutral. They have not necessarily considered the sources from the perspective of either the Appellant or the Respondent. While this was largely because we asked the students to consider both sides of the argument, this can actually be a very beneficial way of approaching your analysis and research. Such an approach allows you to understand the nuances of the law and to be in a strong position when it comes to argument construction. Argument construction is the point in your preparation when you need to begin thinking about how you may *use* the authorities that you have identified and where your discussion of the law and of your particular authorities will begin to become less neutral. You will, at this point, need to start to focus on the specific interests of the position you have been allocated, be it Appellant or Respondent.

PRELIMINARY CONSIDERATIONS FOR CONSTRUCTING A SKELETON ARGUMENT

When beginning to construct an argument generally, and more specifically, when constructing a skeleton argument, there are three main areas to consider. These are:

- **Your overarching argument.** You need to be clear about what your overarching argument is. This is something that we recommended you begin to identify and ensure you are clear on when analysing the problem question on page 8. If you know what your overarching point is, then you can begin to construct arguments that will contribute to developing it.
- **Submissions.** Think about the individual arguments that you will need to make to the court in order to develop your overarching point. These are known as submissions. Your argument must have clarity and be logical so that the judge can follow it. Submissions simply reflect smaller, individual arguments that go towards your overarching argument. You will see below that we suggest three submissions per ground as a general rule of thumb, but there will be times when this is not suitable.

  For example, if your overarching point was that Manchester United Football Club is a successful football club, you might make the following three submissions to support that point. One, they have won more Premier League titles than any other domestic team. Two, they have won multiple European titles. Three, some of the world's most famous and expensive football players have played or now play for the club. For each submission, you would find an authority to support your point.
- **Drafting.** You must draft in a professional and concise way, backing up your arguments with key authorities. You will not write your skeleton argument perfectly first time. Developing a good skeleton argument requires editing and redrafting in order to create a skeleton that will make a good first impression of you as a mooter and team. In developing a good skeleton, you will also then be developing and preparing your argument to present orally.

In addition, there are a number of other considerations you should keep in mind when drafting a skeleton argument. These are:

- **What do you want?** Begin with a clear idea of what your ground of appeal is and what this means you are actually asking the court to do. For instance, are you asking the court to follow a particular precedent or distinguish it? It is easy to get lost in the detail of the law and almost forget what you are asking for.

- **Brevity.** A skeleton argument needs to be informative but it also needs to be brief. Many competitions will have a limit to the length of a skeleton argument so learning to express yourself comprehensively but with brevity is a necessary skill to develop.

- **Best foot forward.** Start with your strongest point. Once you have worked out what your submissions will be, make sure you begin with your best one. Don't build up to it. This will not only signal that your argument has merit, but will give a good first impression to the judge by injecting you with some confidence.

- **Is the law on your side?** You should be clear on where the strengths and weaknesses in your argument lie. This should include whether the law is in support of the point you are seeking to make, or not. If it is not, this is not a disaster. It will simply mean more creative advocating!

- **Terminology.** Make sure you are clear on all the terminology in the question and in the law. You may need to include certain phrases within your skeleton so you need to make sure you understand them. Also, remember, the judge can ask you for a definition at any time!

- **Anticipate.** Begin to think about what the opposition may argue, as well as what questions the judge may ask you in your oral submissions. This will help you to develop a strong skeleton argument, but also will stand you in good stead for preparing for advocating.

- **Authorities and purpose.** You should be clear on all the authorities you are using and what they are being used for. Never include an authority in your skeleton if you cannot justify and explain why it is there.

ARGUMENT CONSTRUCTION: R V HARPER

Keeping in mind the preliminary considerations above, and using research undertaken by Ali and Anna, we constructed a skeleton argument for the Appellant in **R v Harper**.

IN THE SUPREME COURT OF THE UNITED KINGDOM

R v HARPER

Appellant's Skeleton Argument

Senior Counsel for the Appellant shall submit:

1. **Section 1 (1) of the Criminal Attempts Act 1981** requires the Appellant to have engaged in conduct that was 'more than merely preparatory'

---

to the commission of the offence. The Appellant did not go beyond 'mere preparation', as she did not do 'every act which was necessary' for her to achieve the death of John. In particular, she had not aimed the gun. Following *R v Ilyas (Mohammed)* **[1984] 78 Cr App R 17**.

2. The Appellant urges this Court to distinguish the cases of *R v Jones* **[1990] 1 WLR 1057** and **Attorney General's Reference (No. 1 of 1992), [1993] 1 WLR 274**. This is because, unlike the instant case, the former involved an incident whereby the defendant had engaged in extraordinary preparation and aimed the firearm, and the latter relates specifically to attempted rape.

3. To dismiss this appeal would place too wide an interpretation on the phrase 'more than merely preparatory' under **s(1)(1) of the Criminal Attempts Act 1981**. Such an interpretation could lead to mass criminal liability, where mere possession of a weapon could constitute attempted murder. The court should confine such significant liability to facts such as those in *Jones*.

Junior Counsel for the Appellant shall submit:

1. The defence of duress should be made available in cases of attempted murder. The Appellant urges this Court to, on the basis of the facts of the instant case, depart from established precedent in order to make the common law meaningfully reflect that the defence of duress is a 'concession to human frailty'. *See* **R v Howe (Michael Anthony) [1987] 2 WLR 568** and *R v Gotts (Benjamin)* **[1992] 2 AC 412**.

2. The Appellant satisfies the requirements of duress, as set out by the House of Lords in *R v Graham (Paul Anthony)* **[1982] 1 WLR 294** and *R v Hasan (Aytach)* **[2005] UKHL 22**. In particular, the Appellant was directed to carry out a specific crime; was subject to an immediate and personal threat of death; and, given the fact that she was kidnapped, beaten and robbed by the gang, that threat was sufficient to 'overbear the ordinary powers of human resistance'. The Appellant had in no way purposely associated with criminal activity.

3. The Law Commission has unequivocally recommended that the defence of duress be made available in cases of attempted murder. *See:* **Murder, manslaughter and infanticide, Law Com No. 304**. Parliament has failed to seize the opportunity to improve the law in this regard. In the face of Parliament's silence, it is the duty of this court to resolve the matter.

The Appellant respectfully requests that this appeal be allowed.

Senior Counsel: Dr Sarah Cooper   **Junior Counsel**: Dr Scarlett McArdle

RESPONDENT SKELETON ARGUMENT

A clear and accurate skeleton argument is the product of systematic and (often) lengthy analysis, research and editing. To demonstrate this, below we break-down the approach taken by Ali and Anna in order to produce the Respondent's skeleton argument.

Senior Respondent

The ground of appeal that Ali was working on was:

> **The trial judge misdirected the jury in directing them that an act constituting attempted murder had been committed.**

As the Respondent, Ali is arguing against this point, which will mean his over-arching point will be:

> **The trial judge *was correct* in his direction to the jury that an act constituting attempted murder had been committed.**

From Ali's analysis of both the problem question and the ground of appeal, and his research, Ali determined that he needed to make the following 'points' in order to make his overarching argument:

> - This requirement was satisfied when A made the statement and took the gun. The only reason the murder didn't come to fruition is because the crime was interrupted by the police.
> - The actus reus is satisfied if A merely embarked on the commission of the offence (A-G's Reference No. 1 of 1992 [1993] 1 WLR 274).
> - Direct intent can be inferred from the fact that A took the gun and prepared to aim it, and made a statement that indicated she was about to kill the victim. The fact that she denied moral responsibility is irrelevant.

- Dismissing the appeal would act as a useful deterrent to people who attempt criminal activity because it would narrow the requirement for the actus reus. It is also necessary for the law to become stricter on those who are willing to sacrifice the lives of others in exchange for their own. In addition, an unconditional discharge is too lenient a sentence for a defendant who has been convicted of attempting the most serious crime in existence.

Notably Ali has not included within his 'points' all of the authorities that he considered to be important in his research. This does not necessarily mean that the omitted authorities are not useful, but rather Ali rethought his approach once it came to actually constructing his argument. This does not mean that any of his research work will have been unnecessary or wasted. He now knows the area of law well enough to be confident in which sources should be included as authorities in his arguments. Any that he does not include could possibly arise later in the skeleton for the other side or the judge may question Ali on them. If this were to happen, then he would be fully prepared.

After developing these initial 'points', Ali then ordered them and began to think about how they might be grouped together. This enabled him to develop his submissions. As a general rule of thumb, we advise students to focus upon having three submissions. These will often be two legal points and one point of public policy. This is just a general rule, however, and there may be times when more or fewer submissions are appropriate. It may also be the case that a number of legal issues need to be argued. If this happens, then legal arguments should always take priority over a point of policy.

Ali grouped his points into three general points and connected them with authorities. These then became the following submissions:

1. Actus reus. Points 1 and 2. SR will refer to R v Jones and A-G's Reference No. 1 of 1992.

2. Mens rea. Point 3.

3. Policy argument. Point 4.

Ali has very much maintained the structure of establishing a crime; is *actus reus* present and is *mens rea* present, as well as seeking to develop a point of policy. This shows an understanding of the law and what the court will need to be satisfied in order to reject the appeal.

Junior Respondent

The ground of appeal that Anna was working on was:

> **The trial judge misdirected the jury in his direction that duress was no defence to attempted murder.**

Acting for the Respondent, Anna's overarching argument needed to be:

> **The trial judge *was correct* in his direction to the jury that duress was no defence to attempted murder.**

Anna developed the following 'points' as being central to her overarching argument:

- Duress is not a defence for attempted murder offences.
- She had the free will to deny and not accept to take the gun.
- Should she place her life above her friend's?
- Allowing duress for attempted murder offences will lead to allowing the defence for murder.
- Her actions can be seen as an act of selfishness.
- There was no evidence that she would be killed or seriously harmed.
- Her words show her intention of her future actions.

You will notice that Anna has continued to take quite a neutral approach, even at this stage. This was in order to try and help develop well-rounded arguments that responded to the potential arguments for the opposition. Anna's points are also still quite focused on the facts and it is only once she develops them into submissions that we see the inclusion of more law and legal principles. This simply shows a different approach to Ali and is a good example of how there is no 'right' way of approaching the construction of an argument. It is something that students need to learn to find their own way of working on.

Anna then ordered her points and began to think about how they might be grouped together. This enabled her to develop her submissions. She, too, developed three submissions and connected them with authorities. These were as follows:

1. The appellant could have declined, instead she accepted the gun and her words expressed her intentions (R v Gotts (Benjamin) [1992] 2 AC 412).

2. Define duress – the defence of duress is not applicable to attempted murder or murder cases. (The defence of duress should be made available in cases of attempted murder. The Appellant urges this Court to, on the basis of the facts of the instant case, depart from established precedent in order to make the common law meaningfully reflect that the defence of duress is a 'concession to human frailty'. *See*: R v Howe (Michael Anthony) [1987] 2 WLR 568, R v Gotts (Benjamin) [1992] 2 AC 412).

3. How can one evaluate the importance of one's life? The defence of duress has been disliked by most judges as should not be allowed in order to protect the public. R v Graham (Paul Anthony) [1982] 1 WLR 294 (whether the defendant could have resisted to the threats as a sober person of reasonable firmness would have acted under the same circumstances).

Again, it becomes clear that Anna has not included all of the authorities that she uncovered in her research. At this stage, she appears to be focusing on having one 'key' authority for each of her submissions. Her previous work will stand her in good stead, however, for further developing her argument and in responding to challenges from the opposition and from the judge.

After completing their points and submissions, we directed the students to draft a skeleton argument. This often requires polishing of language and ensuring that the points being made are being expressed as clearly as possible. From this construction and further drafting, Ali and Anna produced the following draft skeleton argument.

IN THE SUPREME COURT OF THE UNITED KINGDOM

R v. Harper

Respondent's Skeleton Argument

Senior Counsel for the Respondent shall submit:

Ground One:

1. The appellant has committed the actus reus of attempted murder. By taking the gun and preparing to aim it, the appellant has satisfied the requirement in *s1(1) of the Criminal Attempts Act 1981* for the actus reus to be more than merely preparatory.
2. The appellant had the aim and purpose to commit murder, which satisfies the mens rea of attempted murder. This is proved by the fact that the appellant took the gun and made a statement confirming the victim was about to die at her hands.
3. Dismissing this appeal would clarify the legal position of the actus reus in attempt cases. It would also act as a useful deterrent to those who attempt to commit a crime. Allowing this appeal purely on moral grounds would be wrong as all the actus reus and mens rea requirements in s1(1) are satisfied.

Junior Counsel for the Respondent shall submit:

Ground Two:

1. The appellant had the free will to not respond to the threats and decide not to put her friend's life in danger; however, she did not and therefore cannot use duress as a defence as in the case of **R v Gotts (Benjamin) [1992] 2 AC 412**.
2. The defence of duress is not applicable for attempted murder and murder crimes. Morals and law do not allow a person to take or attempt to take another person's life even at the price of his own as established in the case of **R v Howe (Michael Anthony) [1987] 2 WLR 568**.
3. The appellant's actions were selfish; she or anyone else should not evaluate whether their life is more important than someone else's and thus does not satisfy the requirements for a defence of duress as shown in the case of **R v Graham (Paul Anthony) [1982] 1 WLR 294**.

The Respondent respectfully requests that this appeal be dismissed.

Senior Counsel: Mr. Ali Kazi   **Junior Counsel:** Ms. Anna Hajilari

EDITING DRAFT SKELETON ARGUMENTS

The skeleton constructed by Ali and Anna is 'good' for a number of reasons. First, they have used appropriate headings, labels and titles, and other such formalities like providing their names and clearly dividing the arguments relevant to each ground of appeal. Their skeleton argument is presented in a professional way. Second, their submissions are brief, understandable and relevant to the grounds of appeal. In addition, Ali's submissions directly apply the law to the facts of the instant case, and Anna's submissions include citations to relevant authorities. Third, their arguments fit on to one page, which is often a requirement in many mooting competition rules. In short, their skeleton argument 'looks' good and makes for a good first draft.

However, improvement is always possible. When constructing a skeleton argument you should always be prepared to construct multiple drafts and conduct careful editing. Below is an edited version of Ali and Anna's skeleton, which aims to improve the quality of their arguments and drafting. Under each edited submission we explain the rationale for our edits.

You should take some time to compare and contrast Ali and Anna's skeleton to the edited skeleton argument. Once you have done that, consider that the edited skeleton argument may look significantly different to Ali and Anna's, but it largely built upon their core arguments, whether they be as part of their final argument construction or through earlier research. You will note, in addition to making substantive edits, that the edited skeleton also emboldens authorities, italicises Latin words and phrases, and capitalises the terms 'Respondent' and 'Appellant'. These are stylistic choices that improve the overall professional look of the skeleton.

The edited skeleton argument is, in short, simply more sophisticated. Sophisticated drafting is a skill that is developed over time and with lots of practice.

IN THE SUPREME COURT OF THE UNITED KINGDOM

R v Harper

Respondent's Skeleton Argument

Senior Counsel for the Respondent shall submit:

Ground One:

1. As required by **Section 1 (1) of the Criminal Attempts Act 1981** the Appellant engaged in conduct that is 'more than merely preparatory' to the commission of the offence. The Appellant's relevant conduct was taking the gun and preparing to aim it. This court should follow *R v Jones* **[1990] 1 WLR 1057** and **Attorney General's Reference (No. 1 of 1992), [1993] 1 WLR 274.**

Ali was correct to focus his first submission on the actus reus of attempted murder because it is the focus of the first ground of appeal. The edits to his submission seek to improve the clarity of his argument. It is good form to set out what the law is first before going on to apply it to the facts. It is also important to make it clear which authorities you will be relying on to make your submission. The edited skeleton indicates that the advocate will be relying on Jones and A-G Reference No. 1 to make the point that the Appellant went beyond 'mere preparation'.

2. The offence of attempted murder requires that a defendant intends to kill. *See* **Section 1 (1) of the Criminal Attempts Act 1981.** The Appellant's intention to kill John is demonstrated by, *inter alia*, her taking possession of a loaded gun and making a statement to the effect that John was going to be killed in the course of her actions. This reflects the circumstances in *Jones.*

For his second submission, Ali elected to prove that the mens rea requirement of attempted murder was also satisfied in the Appellant's case. Although mens rea is not the focus of the ground of appeal, this is an acceptable argument because both actus reus and mens rea must be satisfied in order for the conviction to stand. Moreover, the ground of appeal could be considered relatively vague and it is best to be over-prepared than not. If the judge did not want to hear the mooter's representations on this argument, the mooter would simply move on to their third submission. We provide more advice on this eventuality on pages 179–180. Again, the edits to this submission ensured the law was set out clearly before it was applied to the facts of R v Harper, and that the case law to be relied upon was cited.

3. The Respondent urges this Court to dismiss this appeal and clarify the law with regards to the required *actus reus* for attempted murder; confirming the rulings made in ***Jones*, Attorney General's Reference (No. 1 of 1992), [1993] 1 WLR 274**; and *R v Ilyas* **(Mohammed) [1984] 78 Cr App R 17.**

Ali attempted to construct a non-legal argument for his third submission. This approach is perfectly acceptable, particularly as the Supreme Court is concerned with questions that are of general and significant public importance. The edits to his third submission simply polish his argument. Ali rightly says that the court should clarify the law and dismiss the appeal; the edited version does the same thing but in a more formal way. First, the edited version underscores the fact that the mooter is there to persuade the court to the view of his or her client, whether they be the Appellant or Respondent. It is therefore more persuasive (and polite!) to 'urge' the court to make a certain determination rather than bluntly say the court would be 'wrong' to disagree with you. Second, the edited skeleton makes it clear what particular line of precedent the Respondent would like the court to clarify and affirm. These changes improve on Ali's somewhat generic reference to morality. Vague references are not helpful to judges.

Junior counsel for the Respondent shall submit:

Ground Two:
1. The defence of duress is not available to defendants charged with the offence of attempted murder. This is a long-term precedent first stated obiter by the House of Lords in **R v Howe (Michael Anthony) [1987] 2 WLR 568** and affirmed in **R v Gotts (Benjamin) [1992] 2 AC 412** and **R v Hasan (Aytach), [2005] UKHL 22**. The Respondent urges this Court to follow this line of precedent because attempted murder requires proof of 'an even more evil intent' than actual murder, and no one should value their own life over another's.

The edited skeleton changes Anna's first submission so that her strongest argument, namely that precedent has for a long time dictated that duress is not available in cases of attempted murder, is the focus of her overall argument. It is also the argument that falls most squarely within the second ground of appeal. The edited skeleton adds to the authority already cited by Anna and notes that the precedent has emanated from the House of Lords. These changes are made to increase support for the submission and signal the level of persuasiveness that the line of precedent should be afforded by the Supreme Court in the instant case. It also incorporates a quote related to the House of Lords' rationale for taking this approach to the availability of duress, namely that attempted murder requires an even more evil intent than actual murder and it is wrong for a person to value their own life over another's. This terminology is taken direct from the judgment in Howe.

2. Even if the defence of duress was available to the Appellant, she does not satisfy the requirements of the defence, as set out by the House of Lords in **R v Graham (Paul Anthony) [1982] 1 WLR 294** and *Hasan*. In particular, the gang's threats to the Appellant were not sufficient to 'overbear the ordinary powers of human resistance'.

The edited skeleton has replaced Anna's second submission in order to anticipate what the Appellant might argue, namely that the court should widen the applicability of duress to cases of attempted murder and find that Harper satisfies both the historical and most recently articulated requirements for the defence, as set out in the cases of Graham and Hasan respectively. Not acknowledging this likely 'plan of attack' by the Appellant would put the Respondent advocate at a disadvantage.

3. This Court should dismiss this appeal and affirm the approach taken in *Howe* and *Gotts*. Parliament has declined the opportunity to make duress available to the offence of attempted murder, and this Court should not take a course of action that contradicts the will of Parliament. *See* **Murder, manslaughter and infanticide, Law Com No. 304**.

Anna also elected to engage in a more policy-oriented argument in her third submission. The edits to her submission seek to inject more clarity. First, the edited skeleton makes it clear what precedent the Respondent seeks the court to rely on and how. Second, it makes use of an authority Anna discovered in the course of her research, namely the Law Commission Report recommending that duress be applicable in cases of attempted murder. It is likely the Appellant will use the Law Commission's recommendation to urge the court to overrule the precedent in Howe and Gotts, so the edited skeleton constructs an argument that uses Parliament's failure to act on the report's recommendations to the Respondent's advantage; warning the court that it should not act to contradict the will of Parliament.

The Respondent respectfully requests that this appeal be dismissed.

Senior Counsel: Mr. Ali Kazi   **Junior Counsel:** Ms. Anna Hajilari

THINKING AHEAD

When considering the approaches taken by Ali and Anna in the construction of their arguments, both show a clear desire to look ahead beyond the task of writing the skeleton argument.

Ali considered that once you had completed your research and begun to apply the law to the scenario in front of you, then the above tasks are often able to fall into place in a relatively straightforward manner. A key desire of Ali's was to ensure that he was confident on the law all round, rather than simply from one perspective. This way he was confident that he should not be surprised by anything that arises, whether from the judge or from the opposition. Such an approach of being aware of the argument for the other side in quite an explicit manner is reflected in the approach taken by Ali. In beginning his work on argument construction, he quite explicitly begins to consider each side. He immediately begins writing from the perspective of the Appellant and Respondent.

This is quite different to Anna, who maintains quite a neutral approach initially, in seeking to consider the different points as a whole for the ground of appeal. Although different approaches, both students are actually seeking to achieve the same outcome; they are looking for an overall understanding of the law and the arguments that means they understand the perspective of both sides.

This is a useful approach to take, as it begins to prepare you for the task of addressing the arguments of the opposing side and also responding to the judge. It is good practice when developing your argument to begin to consider what the other side may seek to argue and also what sort of a response you may encounter from the judge, and both students have sought to incorporate such preparation into the development of their arguments.

BEING CRITICAL

As part of constructing your argument and preparing to moot, thinking critically about your argument will allow you to further prepare and be aware of what you might face from the opposition or from the judge. Such critique will involve identifying the strengths and weaknesses of each submission and identifying, from this assessment, what the judge and opposing counsel might seek to state and/or question in response to each submission.

Often the best way to do this is consider what questions you might be asked in relation to each ground of appeal and/or submission. Below we provide some possible questions that we would ask Ali and Anna about their submissions for the Respondent in **R v Harper**. We would ask these sorts of questions to test their wider knowledge, and the strength of their arguments.

Read the questions carefully and consider what answers Ali and Anna could give. In later chapters, we consider how mooters can approach answering both case-specific and more general questions. For now, we simply want to introduce you to the types of questions judges might ask. As you will see, judicial intervention is likely to stretch beyond the facts of the problem scenario and the authorities included in the skeleton arguments, so advocates must be prepared to engage with the judge about the law in a holistic way.

Ground One

Is the case of Jones distinguishable from the instant case on the basis that Harper did not engage in the same level of preparation as Jones did?

What does it mean when a case is labelled 'Attorney General's Reference'?

What specific question did the Attorney General refer to the court in the case you cite?

Must a defendant do every act necessary to complete the offence, in order to go beyond mere preparation?

Does the phrase 'more than merely preparatory' in section 1 of the Criminal Attempts Act 1981 have an exhaustive definition?

Are the acts undertaken by the Appellant too remote from the contemplated offence?

Would ruling in favour of the Respondent set the bar too low for committing a criminal attempt in this context?

Ground Two

Is this court bound to follow the decisions of the House of Lords?

What particular facts in the instant case justify a departure from such an established precedent?

Does the Appellant advocate for the defence of duress to be available to all charges of attempted murder or just those reflecting the facts of the instant case?

Did the court in Hasan make any reference to the applicability of duress to attempted murder cases?

Is this court or Parliament obliged to follow the recommendations of the Law Commission?

How many times has the Law Commission recommended that the law with regards to the availability of the defence of duress be amended?

Can you give the court an example of when this court or its predecessor has made a significant change to the law in the absence of action by Parliament?

SUMMARY

Constructing a clear and logical argument that addresses the grounds of appeal in a comprehensive way, which accounts for both their strengths and weaknesses, is vital to preparing to moot successfully.

It is also important to remember that the construction of your skeleton argument and your critical assessment of it is just one step (albeit a significant one) in preparing to moot. Once you have completed this process it is time to develop your extended oral presentation. We provide some guidance on how to do this in the final chapter of this book.

Conclusion

In this chapter, we have shown you how to analyse, research and construct an argument in relation to the moot problem presented by the fictitious case of **R v Harper**.

2

TORT LAW

INTRODUCTION

In this chapter, we will show you how to analyse, research and construct an argument in relation to the moot problem presented by the fictitious case of **Live and Loud Ltd v Andrew Jones-Hacker**. This is a tort law themed moot problem question.

In this question, Ali undertook the roles of Senior Appellant and Senior Respondent, and Anna prepared for the roles of Junior Appellant and Junior Respondent.

ANALYSIS

THE PROBLEM QUESTION

A ## IN THE COURT OF APPEAL (CIVIL DIVISION)

LIVE AND LOUD LTD **B**

V

ANDREW JONES-HACKER **C**

D Andrew Jones and James Hacker became civil partners in January 2013, but by late 2014 their relationship had become strained after rumours of Andrew's infidelity circulated amongst their friends on social media. Andrew moved out of the couple's home in November 2014 and went to stay with a friend, Kate. Since Andrew had moved out, the couple had texted each other every day about the well-being and living arrangements of their dog, Boxer.

E James was a sound engineer at a large concert venue in Birmingham, which was owned by Live and Loud Ltd. On 10 December 2014, he was working as an engineer at the largest concert of the year: The Pop Goes Christmas Extravaganza. The concert involved lots of different pop singers and drew a crowd of up to 12,000 people. It was also broadcast live on television. Midway through the concert, a large fire started because of faulty wiring in the main lights structure present on the stage. The concert hall quickly filled with smoke as the fire spread. Everyone inside rushed to escape.

Andrew, who was out on a date at a bar in Birmingham at the time of the concert, heard news of the fire via Twitter. Concerned that James was working at the event, Andrew video-called him from his smart phone. James answered the video call, and Andrew could see he was coughing. His face appeared blackened, but James was not visibly burnt. The video call paused every few seconds and was blurred because of the smoke. Andrew could not clearly hear what James was saying due to the level of noise in the hall. After the video call disconnected for the fifth time, Andrew received a text from James saying 'OK. Trying 2 get out X.'

Leaving his date, Andrew rushed down to the concert venue in time to see James being stretchered on to an ambulance. He was suffering from severe smoke inhalation and second degree burns to his hands. The paramedics intubated James to help him breathe. James was comatose for the next 48 hours. Subsequently doctors informed Andrew that James' brain had been starved of oxygen for too long, and that he would never recover beyond a permanent vegetative state. Andrew kept a constant vigil at James' bedside, and held his hand as his life support machine was disconnected. James died soon after.

F Andrew is now suffering from PTSD. He brought a claim as a secondary victim for nervous shock against Live and Loud Ltd, who accepted liability for James' injuries.

At first instance, Fallon J found that Andrew could claim as a secondary victim on the grounds that:

G 1. As a spouse, it was clear that Andrew had a close tie of love and affection with the person injured, namely James.
2. On the basis of what Andrew saw on the video call, Andrew qualified as a secondary victim.

Live and Loud Ltd now appeal to the Court Appeal (Civil Division) on the grounds that:

H 1. Andrew did not have a sufficiently 'close tie of love and affection' with James at the time of the incident and therefore does not qualify as a secondary victim. ***Alcock v Chief Constable of South Yorkshire* [1992] 1 AC 310**.
I 2. Alternatively, the lower court placed too broad an interpretation on the dicta from *Alcock*. Andrew was not sufficiently proximate to the incident via the video call.

UNDERSTANDING THE BASICS OF THE PROBLEM QUESTION

Again we will begin by analysing the moot problem question. Below you will find a list of features identified by the relevant letter in the problem question above.

A **COURT**

Live and Loud Ltd v Jones-Hacker is in the UK Court of Appeal Civil Division. The Court of Appeal is bound by the decisions of the Supreme Court and its predecessor, the House of Lords. The Court of Appeal has a system of precedent with regard to its own decisions. Following the case of *Young v Bristol Aeroplane Co Ltd* [1944] KB 718, the Court of Appeal is typically bound by its own decisions, except in the following three circumstances:

1. Where its own previous decisions conflict. The Court of Appeal must choose which decision to follow.
2. Where to follow a decision of its own would conflict with a decision of the UK Supreme Court (or House of Lords).

3. Where an earlier decision was given *per incuriam* (through lack of due regard for the law or facts).

B APPELLANT

The first name indicates who is appealing to the appeal court. In this case, Live and Loud Ltd are appealing the points of law to the Court of Appeal after being found liable for Andrew's injuries in the court of first instance.

C RESPONDENT

The second name indicates who is responding to the appeal. In this case, Andrew Jones-Hacker is responding to the appeal. In effect, in this case, the Respondent is asking the Court of Appeal to affirm the lower court's decision.

D INCIDENT FACTS: RELATIONSHIP

The first paragraph sets out facts that mostly pertain to the quality of the relationship between Andrew and James. This may not usually seem significant, but in this area, the relationship shared by the Respondent and deceased relates directly to the grounds of appeal.

E INCIDENT FACTS: FIRE

The next three paragraphs set out facts that relate mostly to the particular incident that has happened here, namely the fire. You will note that this relates to the second ground of appeal, i.e. whether Andrew had sufficient proximity to the incident.

F INITIAL CLAIM

This explains the initial tortious claim that Andrew filed against Live and Loud Ltd.

G IMMEDIATE PROCEDURAL HISTORY

This tells you what has happened in the court directly below the court in which the moot problem question is in. For example, in **Live and Loud Ltd v Jones-Hacker**, the case was last heard in the High Court.

H GROUND ONE OF THE APPEAL

This ground 'belongs' to Senior Counsel for both the Appellant and the Respondent, which in this case is Ali. The Appellant will argue for the appeal, whereas the Respondent will argue against. In **Live and Loud Ltd v Jones-Hacker**, the Senior Appellant will argue Andrew was *not* a secondary victim as he did not share a sufficiently 'close tie of love and affection' with James at the time of the incident. Conversely, the Respondent will argue that such close ties of love and affection did exist and therefore Andrew does qualify as a secondary victim. Note that the case of *Alcock* is cited in a general way in this ground of appeal. This means that Senior Counsel for both sides must use this case.

GROUND TWO OF THE APPEAL

This ground 'belongs' to Junior Counsel for both the Appellant and the Respondent, which in this case is Anna. The Appellant will argue for the appeal, whereas the Respondent will argue against. In **Live and Loud Ltd v Jones-Hacker**, the Junior Appellant will argue that Andrew was not sufficiently proximate to the incident via the video call. The Respondent, on the other hand, will argue that there was sufficient proximity for Andrew to qualify as a secondary victim. Note that *Alcock* is cited again, but this time in a very specific way that will require Junior Counsel for both sides to address the breadth of its interpretation in the lower court. The Junior Appellant will argue the prior court's interpretation of *Alcock* was too broad in this case, and the Junior Respondent will oppose this. Also note that the second of ground appeal is an alternative argument. This means it is a 'safety net' of sorts for the Appellant. If the Appellant loses on ground one, they will rely on the argument set forth in ground two. Either way, the view of the Appellant will be that Andrew does not qualify as a secondary victim.

SUMMARISING THE CASE

We will now summarise the moot question in preparation for analysing the problem in more detail.

Below is the summary constructed by Ali:

- *James and Andrew were civil partners whose relationship had become strained due to rumours of Andrew's infidelity. This resulted in Andrew moving out of their home, and they only remained in contact to discuss the living arrangements of their dog.*

- *James worked as a sound engineer for Live and Loud Ltd, the Appellant, at a concert venue. On 10 December 2014, he was working at a large concert when faulty wiring on stage caused a fire.*

- *At the time of the concert, Andrew was on a date in a bar and heard about the fire via Twitter. Concerned about James, Andrew tried to video-call him several times but could not hear or see due to the noise level and the smoke from the fire. James sent Andrew a text telling him he was trying to get out.*

- *Andrew arrived at the concert in time to see James being stretchered out. James was in hospital for two days and Andrew stayed at his bedside. James died due to the fact that his brain was starved of oxygen for too long. Andrew now suffers from PTSD and brought a psychiatric injury claim against Live and Loud as a secondary victim.*

- *Andrew's claim was successful at first instance. Live and Loud now appeal on the grounds that Andrew did not have a close tie of love and affection with James, and that he was not sufficiently proximate to the incident.*

Ali attempts to provide a summary that conforms with our general rule of thumb: namely that is useful to construct a summary spanning five bullet points. Ali includes facts that relate directly to the two grounds of appeal, namely facts that go to the nature of the relationship between Andrew and James, and facts that relate to Andrew's proximity to the fire incident. He provides his facts in a chronological order and ends with the legal points that are before the instant court. This is a positive improvement on the summary Ali produced for the criminal law moot question, which was far too detailed. However, Ali's summary could still benefit from further editing in order to make it more 'punchy' to present to the judge.

Below is the summary constructed by Anna:

James and Andrew became civil partners in January 2013; however, by late 2014 their relationship had fallen apart due to Andrew's infidelity, which led Andrew to move out. The pair kept messaging after this time. James was working on one of the biggest concerts of the year in Birmingham, during which a large fire broke out. Andrew was then on a date and hearing the news made him video-call James and seeing him trying to get out with difficulty in breathing. Andrew saw James being carried in an ambulance and was present when his life support machine was disconnected. He now suffers from PTSD and is bringing a claim against Live and Loud Ltd as a secondary victim for nervous shock. They have accepted liability for James' injuries but have appealed on Andrew's claim.

Anna has taken a similar approach to summarising the case as she did with the criminal law problem, in that she has provided a summary written in prose rather than points. Anna has clearly responded to feedback about making sure that she does not overlook fundamental facts. This is shown by her identifying facts relevant to the relationship and to the fire. Yet, like Ali, she includes a number of facts that are unnecessary for a brief case summary. For example, while Ali mentions Andrew received news about the fire on Twitter, Anna includes facts such as James being at work at one of the biggest concerts of the year. All told, both students could be a little more discriminatory in their choice of facts when drafting, which would allow them to bring the more fundamental facts to the forefront of their summaries.

Below is an example of a summary we developed to try and take a middle ground between Ali and Anna's approaches.

- *Andrew and James were separated civil partners. Andrew had moved out of their home, but the pair were in regular contact.*

- *James was caught in a fire while at work.*

- *During the fire, James was in contact with Andrew via video call and text. Andrew went to the scene and saw James being given medical assistance. James later died from his injuries with Andrew at his bedside.*

- *Andrew claimed damages as a secondary victim for PTSD and was successful at first instance.*

- *Live and Loud Ltd now appeal on the basis that Andrew and James had insufficient close ties of love and affection for Andrew to qualify as a secondary victim and that, in the alternative, Andrew was insufficiently proximate to the event to qualify as a secondary victim. The case of* Alcock *is central to this appeal.*

We have followed our general guidance of including key facts and excluding extraneous detail. When constructing the summary, we knew that points needed to be made about the relationship between Andrew and James and the contact between the two men during the fire. This reflects the first and second ground of appeal respectively, as will be seen in the section below. We also knew that we needed to provide references to the history of the claim and the current appeal points before the Court of Appeal. The above summary encompasses all of these key points.

While it is important with a criminal law problem to state the charge and the previous procedural history, in a tort law problem question it is important to identify the particular tortious claim at hand. In this problem, the tort concerned is negligence but this does not form the focus of the claim. Instead, the key point is whether Andrew is able to claim as a secondary victim for negligently inflicted psychiatric injury. This is an important distinction to note in the summary.

UNDERSTANDING YOUR GROUND OF APPEAL

This section considers the argument that each mooter will make. Remember that each mooter will only be allowed to make the argument, and pursue the particular angle, directed in the relevant ground of appeal. The mooter's main choice is about how to present that argument in terms of the interpretation of the law.

The instant grounds of appeal are slightly different to those in the criminal law problem, as they present 'alternative' arguments. This means that the appeal is constructed to give the judge two possible arguments, both of which lead to the same conclusion, namely, that the appeal should be allowed. It is important to recognise this as it may affect the construction of your submissions.

In **Live and Loud Ltd v Jones-Hacker**, the grounds both revolve around Andrew qualifying as a secondary victim. In order to qualify as a secondary victim for nervous shock arising from negligence (a tort), claimants must satisfy certain criteria. Two of these criteria are relevant to the instant appeal. First, Andrew needs to have shared a relationship with James that had sufficiently close ties of love and affection. Second, Andrew needed to have sufficient proximity to the incident surrounding James' death. Live and Loud Ltd, as the Appellant, will be trying to challenge Andrew's status as a secondary victim. The grounds of appeal have been devised to do this in two alternative ways; if one is not satisfied Andrew will lose his status as a secondary victim. The first ground of appeal challenges the quality of the relationship Andrew shared with James. The second ground challenges Andrew's proximity to the incident surrounding James' death, and specifically at the point he was conversing with James via a video call. If the Court of Appeal accepts either argument, Andrew will fail to qualify as a secondary victim. An appeal structured in this way, thus, gives the Appellant two chances of 'winning' the appeal. The Respondent must then argue that both criteria are satisfied in order for Andrew to retain his status as a secondary victim. Neither ground can be ignored.

It should be noted when considering the grounds of appeal that they both, in different ways, make direct mention of the case of *Alcock v Chief Constable for South Yorkshire Police*. In the first ground of appeal, *Alcock* is cited generally. This has been done deliberately. *Alcock* is a leading authority on nervous shock and so is a key case for the mooters to be engaging with. The second ground of appeal, however, uses *Alcock* far more specifically. Junior Counsel are directed on the manner in which *Alcock* should be used. In the area of proximity, Junior Counsel are required to engage in *Alcock's* interpretation of proximity and to consider its particular application in the present case.

While the Appellant will be arguing that the interpretation made by the lower court is too broad, the Respondent will be arguing that it was not, or, of course, that a broad interpretation is appropriate.

As we did with the criminal law question, it is a good idea to clarify your basic points by asking yourself a few simple questions. Below are some examples in the context of **Live and Loud Ltd v Jones-Hacker:**

- Am I arguing for the appeal to be allowed or dismissed?
- Am I arguing that Andrew was or was not a secondary victim?
- Am I arguing that Andrew and James shared a relationship with sufficiently close ties of love and affection, or not?
- Am I arguing that Andrew was, or was not, sufficiently proximate to the incident?
- How am I using *Alcock*, the case cited in the grounds of appeal?

Once you are comfortable with the answers to these questions, you should be in a position to identify search terms that can be used to start your legal research.

SELECTING YOUR RESEARCH TERMS

This section is designed to help you move from analysing the problem question into beginning your research. Again, Ali and Anna were directed to systematically select their research terms, including both obvious and hidden terms.

Below is Ali's attempt for the Senior Appellant and Respondent:

Paragraph	Obvious Research Terms	Hidden Research Terms
1	relationship, infidelity, moved out	husband, wife, partner, spouse, family, friend, special relationship, affair, disagreement, separation, estrangement, divorce, break up
2	working, crowd	employee, worker, staff, people, noise, danger
3	concerned, video call, text, date	worry, alarm, panic, call, text, message, contact

4	constant vigil, bedside, held his hand, rushed, never recover, ambulance	doctor, hospital, permanently injured, stay, remain, awake, anxiety
5	PTSD, nervous shock, secondary victim	psychiatric illness, psychiatric damage, mental illness, disorder, impairment, shock
6	spouse, love and affection	loving relationship, caring relationship

The vast majority of Ali's terms relate to the nature of the relationship shared by Andrew and James. This shows Ali has paid close attention to his ground of appeal, which questions the closeness of the loving ties between James and Andrew. This is a focused approach that attempts to avoid research that goes 'off track'. Ali's hidden terms consider the sorts of words and phrases that might appear in case law that considers similar legal issues. The hidden terms for paragraph one provide a particularly compelling example of this. These terms show that Ali has appreciated that the quality of other types of relationships, such as those between husband and wife, partner and partner and friends and relatives, may have been questioned in other cases. Ali also shows an awareness for a variety of circumstances that might impact how 'close' and 'loving' individuals are in a relationship, ranging from disagreement to divorce and separation. Ali has attempted to identify appropriate synonyms in areas. For example, in paragraph three, Ali comes up with a number of hidden words to reflect Andrew's concern for James when he was caught in the fire. One thing Ali has not included, which very much should be, is a reference to the case of *Alcock*. This suggests Ali was either too discriminatory in his selection of terms, or considered the inclusion of *Alcock* in his research terms document to be so obvious that he neglected to include it. This latter perspective is understandable, yet we encourage students to take a comprehensive approach to identifying and noting down research terms. This is because it is easy to lose track of key terms and, when given an authority by the problem question, to relegate its importance, rather than embrace its prominence.

Anna continued preparing for the roles of Junior Appellant and Respondent. Again, naturally, these roles will both consider the same terms and focus on the same area at this point in the process. Below is Anna's attempt for the Junior Appellant and Respondent:

Paragraph	Obvious Research Terms	Hidden Research Terms
1	civil partners, January 2013, late 2014, relationship, strained, rumours, infidelity, social media, moved out, text each other every day, well-being and arrangements of their dog	break of trust, end of relationship, kept in touch, constant texting, maintain relationship
2	sound engineer, 10 December 2014, engineer, largest concert of the year, broadcast live on television, mid-way, large fire started, quickly filled with smoke, fire spread, rushed to escape	large responsibility, potential danger, direct access to everyone through television, major disaster, dangerous situations
3	out on a date, at the time of the concert, heard the news, Twitter, concerned, video-called him, answered, could see he was coughing, face, blackened, was not visibly burnt, paused every few seconds, blurred because of the smoke, could not clearly hear, disconnected for the fifth time, text from James, 'OK. Trying 2 get out X'	moved on with his life by dating, received news from indirect source, worried for well-being, wanted to see his face, making sure he is secure, worried as there was a problem with the connection, insisted to the video call as it disconnected five times
4	leaving his date, rushed down, to see James being stretchered on to an ambulance, severe smoke inhalation, second degree burns to his hands, intubated, help him breathe, comatosed, 48 hours, brain, starved from oxygen for too long, never recover beyond a permanent vegetative state, constant vigil, held his hand, life support machine was disconnected, died	abandoned date, care, was present when his partner was carried out, present when he died, close proximity to the outcome of the accident
5	suffering, PTSD, secondary victim, nervous shock, accepted liability for James' injuries	was scared after the accident

Anna's approach is to lift text from the problem question far more comprehensively, and often verbatim. This approach ensures she does not omit key facts; however she could, at first attempt, filter the terms she selects more robustly. The end result of Anna's approach is that she has a lot of terms yet to filter before she can proceed with focused research. For example, Anna includes in her obvious terms many adjectives related to the quality of the relationship shared by Andrew and James. These, however, are not acutely related to the second ground of appeal, but the first. However, as shown in the research section, Anna engages in a very astute categorisation of her terms, namely she groups them according to the tests set out in *Alcock*. This lends support to the notion that there is no single, correct way to analyse a problem question and select research terms. Both analysis and research are malleable concepts that are open to interpretation.

Taking into consideration Ali and Anna's different approaches, below is our attempt at selecting research terms for Senior Counsel and Junior Counsel.

Senior Counsel

Our aim was to focus quite stringently on the core of the ground of appeal. As such we only selected obvious terms and generated hidden terms that could be associated with the quality of the relationship shared between Andrew and James. We also used our pre-existing (but still rudimentary) legal knowledge about negligence and psychiatric damage, in that we recalled the relevance of the Hillsborough Disaster and how that incident generated a series of case law concerning claims for psychiatric damage.

Paragraph	Obvious Research Terms	Hidden Research Terms
1	relationship, infidelity, moved out, civil partners	husband, wife, partner, spouse, affair, separation/ separated, divorce, break-up, text, communicating/ communication/in-touch
2	No terms selected	No terms devised
3	date, concerned, video call, text	care/anxious, contact
4	leaving his date, constant vigil, bedside, held his hand, rushed	loving, caring, concern
5	PTSD, nervous shock, secondary victim	psychiatric damage, Hillsborough
6	spouse, close tie of love and affection, *Alcock*	

Junior Counsel

Again, we were keen to focus on the ground of appeal at hand, namely the proximity that Andrew had to the incident where James was injured, and specifically through the video call. To this end, we selected and generated terms that were closely related to the fire, the communication between the two men during the fire, and Andrew's witnessing of James' injuries once he arrived at the scene and attended the hospital. We used our basic tort knowledge to develop our hidden research terms at points. For instance, we include the phrase 'immediate aftermath' as we know this is a phrase associated with cases where individuals have claimed for nervous shock upon encountering a distressing scene. We also considered terms that might be related to the use of a video call, namely 'technology', 'screen' and 'electronic media'.

Paragraph	Obvious Research Terms	Hidden Research Terms
1		
2	fire, spread, smoke, escape	emergency, danger, at risk
3	video call, twitter, text, not visibly burnt, face appeared blackened	social media, telephone, electronic media, technology, injured/injuries, harm, witness, television, screen
4	stretchered on to ambulance, severe smoke inhalation, second degree burns, intubated, comatose, permanent vegetative state, constant vigil, bedside	hurt/injured/harm, distress, trauma, immediate aftermath
5	PTSD, nervous shock	Hillsborough, psychiatric damage

SUMMARY

In this section, we have shown you how to analyse a tort law moot problem question. We have done this by, first, deconstructing the problem question to highlight its fundamental features. We have then demonstrated approaches to summarising the problem question, interpreting the grounds of appeal and generating initial research terms. We will utilise these research terms in the next section, which focuses on how to carry out appropriate legal research for **Live and Loud Ltd v Andrew Jones-Hacker.**

RESEARCH

This section focuses on how to research the areas of law related to **Live and Loud Ltd v Andrew Jones-Hacker**. This problem question is also a common law-centric problem; however, this time, the case law used is of a civil law nature, and the differences in the relevant case law are far more subtle. This section will concentrate on developing your research skills in identifying, interpreting and applying these civil law cases, as well as developing an understanding of the relevance of the case law to the case at hand.

Before going on to consider the specific research Ali and Anna undertook for this case, you should remind yourself of the preliminary considerations for researchers that we set out on page 14.

RESEARCHING LIVE AND LOUD LTD V ANDREW JONES-HACKER

The rules in relation to **Live and Loud Ltd v Andrew Jones-Hacker** allowed Ali and Anna each to use three cases, any relevant legislation and two 'other' sources.

Before beginning their research, we asked Ali and Anna to categorise the search terms that they had developed at the end of their analysis of the moot problem. They were also asked to explain their rationale behind choosing such categories.

Ground One

Ali generated the following categories:

- General.

- Appellant's case.

- Respondent's case.

While Ali may have been considering this approach to be useful in terms of focusing his arguments for each side, it is likely that at this stage terms and categories would largely be similar for both sides. This approach would have been a quick one for Ali to take and follow through with; however, it does not assist him much in further analysing the problem to begin his research more thoroughly. Ali tends to take quite a 'quick' approach to categorisation.

He prefers to dive into using his search terms and then get going with the body of his legal research. He then later considers more precise categories and further terms, including synonyms and terms and connectors. This is demonstrated by his research trail, which can be seen below:

	Search Terms	Search Criteria	Results	Notes
1	'nervous shock' OR psychiatric and 'secondary victim' and relationship and 'love and affection'	Tort cases sorted by relevance	*Holdich v Lothian Health Board* [2013] CSOH 197 +25 more	Search was not restricted enough to limit results to cases on love and affection. Too many Scottish cases!
2	'nervous shock' or 'psychiatric damage' and 'secondary victim' and loving relationship and 'love and affection' family and partner or spouse or husband or wife	Tort cases sorted by relevance	*Holdich v Lothian Health Board* [2013] CSOH 197 +3 more	Lots of cases from lower courts, not persuasive enough.
3	Brought up a list of significant cases that cited Alcock		*Galli-Atkinson v Seghal* [2003] EWCA Civ 697, *Monk v PC Harrington Ltd* [2008] EWHC 1879, *White v Lidl UK GmbH* [2005] EWHC 871 (QB) +29 more	Important to look at key words and case analysis, as this kind of search won't only come up with cases relating to relationships. Also, focus on cases that actually apply the Alcock principles.

| 4 | Negligence and psychiatric and 'secondary victim' and relationship and 'love and affection' and infidelity or affair and argument or divorce or separation or estrangement or disagreement or dispute | | *Cross v Highlands & Islands Enterprise* [2001] SLT 1060, *Barrett v Enfield lbC* [2001] 2 AC 550 | These results are not relevant, so there are no cases as of today relating to this ground of appeal and relationships which have broken down as in the instant case. |

Ali determined the following three cases as being central to his argument:

- *Alcock v Chief Constable of South Yorkshire* [1992] 1 AC 310.

- *Shorter v Surrey and Sussex Healthcare NHS Trust* [2015] EWHC 614 QB.

- *McFarlane v EE Caledonia Ltd* [1994] 2 All ER 1.

Ground Two

Anna generated the following categories:

- **Close tie of love and affection.**

- **Witness event with own unaided senses.**

- **Proximity to event or its immediate aftermath.**

- **The psychiatric injury must be caused by a shocking event.**

Anna clearly generated these categories after doing some preliminary research about the *Alcock* case, and her research lead her to justify the categories to be reflective of the tests laid down in *Alcock*. Although her aim to be methodical is laudable, it leads her first to include more law than she needs to; her ground of appeal would only address her second and third categories. Second, her approach has led to an awkward phrasing of some of the tests. It appears that Anna did not go direct to the case judgment of the House of Lords or an academic text, but rather used an abbreviated revision source. This is apparent by the wording of her categories. A number of revision sources paraphrase the tests in *Alcock* as above. However, in doing so, they obscure the tests. It is far more appropriate to begin with the judgment itself (or, at very least, a reliable academic textbook such as *Street on Torts* or *Tort Law by* Kirsty Horsey, Erika Rackley). For instance, if Anna had gone to such a reliable source she would have found the current, established phrasing of the tests. These tests were most recently summarised by the House of Lords in the case of *White v Chief Constable for South Yorkshire* [1998] 3 WLR 1509:

> It has become settled that, to establish the necessary proximity, a secondary victim must show (1) a close tie of love and affection to the immediate victim; (2) closeness in time and space to the incident or its aftermath; and (3) perception by sight or hearing, or its equivalent, of the event or its aftermath.

Anna's categories are certainly similar to those set out by the House of Lords in *White*. Anna's second category, for example, relates to the third strand in *White*, as both link to the claimant's perception of the incident. Anna's phrasing of this issue as 'witness event with own unaided senses', however, gives the impression that the test requires that a secondary victim must witness the event in person; however, this is not in keeping with the phrasing of the court in *White*. In fact, Anna's phrasing stems from a 1983 case, *McLoughlin v O'Brian* [1983] 1 AC 410. This case is very much connected with *White* and *Alcock*, as you will see below. All this goes to show how the common law in relation to secondary victims is quite particular, in the sense that it has slowly evolved with subtle but distinct changes to the language used to determine a secondary victim. This evolution is accounted for in the case summaries we provide below. This particularity, however, presses the need for a mooter to be very precise in the terms they use.

The problems with Anna's initial categorisation do not fundamentally hinder her research. She is still able to logically generate useful sources. Interestingly, she bypasses her categorisation and returns to using the wording of the ground of appeal, specifically the terms 'secondary victim' and 'proximity'. This can be seen from her research trail:

Begin with Cases.

Step One: **Log-on to Westlaw UK and conduct a free text search of the case law using the terms 'secondary victims' AND 'proximity'.**
This produced 207 results.

Step Two: **Narrow the results by topic area, i.e. those relevant to tort law.**
This narrowed my list to 127 results.

Step Three: **Narrow the results by court to those in the Court of Appeal.**
This narrowed to 33 results.

Step Four: **Consider cases which cited *Alcock v Chief Constable for South Yorkshire* and *McLoughlin v O'Brian*.**
Journal articles under the same case: look at relevant key words – shock induced psychiatric injury, damage limitation.

Conduct a further search of the case law.

Step One: **Search within the cases section of Westlaw UK. Search for 'Alcock test' within the free text option.**
This produced 207 results.

Step Two: **Narrow results by searching for 'video call' within the results. This then narrowed to 12 results. When further narrowed by topic area to 'Tort', 10 results were released. This led to finding the case *McFarlane v Wilkinson*.**

Conduct a search of the case law in LexisNexis.

Step One: **Search within the cases section of LexisNexis. Search for 'secondary victims' AND 'proximity' within the free text option.**
This produced 185 results.

Step Two: **Narrow results by topics of 'Tort and Delict – Negligence'. This narrowed the results to 173 results. This led to the case of *Taylor v Novo*.**

Conduct a search of journals in LexisNexis.

Step One: **Search within the journals section of LexisNexis. Search for 'secondary victims' AND 'proximity' within the free text option.**
This produced 42 results.

After searching through the results, this led to Donal Nolan, 'Horrifying events and their consequences: clarifying the operation of the Alcock criteria'.

From this research, Anna selected the following key sources:

- *Galli-Atkinson v Seghal* [2003] EWCA Civ. 697.
- *Alcock v Chief Constable of South Yorkshire* [1992] 1 AC 310.
- *McLoughlin v O'Brian* [1983] 1 AC 410.
- *Taylor v A Novo* (UK) Ltd [2013] EWCA Civ. 194.
- Donal Nolan, Horrifying events and their consequences: clarifying the operation of the Alcock criteria, (2014) 30(3) PN 176.

Anna eventually narrowed down this list, rejecting *Taylor*. This is shown by her submissions on page 77. This was done after further analysis of the sources.

Ali and Anna's selection of authorities reflects that the two grounds of appeal are closely related. Both students have chosen some of the same authorities to argue their distinct grounds of appeal. This does not show any misunderstanding; in fact it shows that they have (eventually through their analysis of the authorities) identified that their grounds of appeal are interlinked, in that they are both concerned with Andrew's qualification as a secondary victim. The first ground of appeal deals with one criterion, and ground two deals with another. Obviously, key cases will have likely dealt with both criteria, although probably to varying extents. The obvious example of this is *Alcock*.

SUMMARISING THE RELEVANCE OF AUTHORITIES

Below we have created a summary of each source selected by Ali and Anna. These summaries include a factual synopsis and guidance on the significance of each case generally and in relation to each ground of the appeal. These summaries are presented in chronological order to show the subtle evolution of the case law, and, thus, the overlap between the two grounds of appeal. These tables show a slightly different way to summarising the relevance of authorities, in comparison to our approach in the criminal law chapter. Still, items included in the criminal law chapter summaries, such as 'persuasiveness', are not to be forgotten.

McLoughlin v O'Brian [1983] 1 AC 410

Presiding Court	This is a House of Lords case.
Synopsis	The claimant's husband and three children were involved in a car crash caused by O'Brian's negligent driving. The claimant was told of the accident by a friend when she, the claimant, was two miles away. The claimant arrived at the hospital and was told one of her children had died, and then saw her other family members before they had been properly cleaned up. The claimant suffered severe shock, depression and a change of personality. She claimed as a secondary victim for those injuries.
	The House of Lords extended the class of persons who would be considered proximate to the event (and thus a secondary victim) to those who come within the 'immediate aftermath' of the event. This included the claimant.
Relevance to the Grounds of Appeal	This case significantly changed the law. Prior to this case, the conditions for liability to a secondary victim generally required that a claimant be present at the scene, or at least very close by, so they could perceive what happened with their own unaided senses. This case represents a widening of the law in relation to proximity. Secondary victims can now be people who experience 'the immediate aftermath' of a traumatic event.
	This case therefore relates acutely to the second ground of appeal in that it questions whether Andrew's presence at the scene of the fire could fall within *McLoughlin*'s 'immediate aftermath'.
	It has less relevance for the first ground of appeal as sufficient closeness of relationship between the claimant and the primary victim in this case was never an issue.

Alcock v Chief Constable of South Yorkshire [1992] 1 AC 310

Presiding Court This is a House of Lords case.

Synopsis This case arose from the disaster that occurred at Hillsborough football stadium, where 95 people died and over 400 were injured. Poor directing on the part of South Yorkshire Police caused the incident. The event was broadcast live on television, so many people, other than those present at the scene, saw the traumatic scenes. The claimants' actions in this case were for psychiatric illness ensuing from what had happened to their relatives who were in attendance at the stadium.

In this case, the House of Lords clarified some key issues related to the concept of a 'secondary victim'.

Relevance to the Grounds of Appeal This is now the leading case about who can claim as a secondary victim for psychiatric harm. It is well documented that the House of Lords adopted a pragmatic approach to psychiatric harm; although Lord Oliver expressed concern that the law was not satisfactory and Parliamentary intervention might be warranted.

In relation to the first ground of appeal, the court refused to prescribe rigid categories of 'secondary victim' claimants in nervous shock cases. They held that there must generally be a 'close tie of love and affection' between the claimant and primary victim. In Andrew's case, his relationship with James will come under scrutiny. The court will be looking to establish whether a separated civil partner can qualify as a secondary victim.

In relation to the second ground of appeal, the court ruled that there should be a degree of proximity in time and space between the claimant and the incident. The claimant must normally witness the incident or come upon its 'immediate aftermath'. In relation to Andrew, this means his perception of the events (via video phone and at the scene) will be scrutinised to consider whether it meets the required level of proximity.

McFarlane v Wilkinson EE Caledonia Ltd [1994] 2 All ER 1

Presiding Court This is a Court of Appeal (Civil Division) case.

Synopsis This case arose from the Piper Alpha disaster in which a fire broke out in an oil rig resulting in the death of 164 workers. The claimant witnessed the destruction from aboard a support vessel that was sent to rescue survivors. He was not involved in the rescue effort and was far enough away from the burning rig to be in no personal danger.

The claimant argued he was a secondary victim, but the Court of Appeal rejected his claim. As a bystander only, it was not foreseeable that he would suffer such shock.

Relevance to the Grounds of Appeal This case sought to limit a gap left open by *Alcock*. In *Alcock*, Lord Ackner suggested that in cases of exceptional horror even a bystander unrelated to the victim could be able to recover as a secondary victim, if they were a reasonably strong-nerved individual.

In this case, the Court of Appeal did not wholly reject the idea that bystanders could recover, but held that the psychiatric harm would have to be reasonably foreseeable in the circumstances. It could not be shown that a man of ordinary fortitude in a similar position would have been so affected; consequently, the injuries being unforeseeable, McFarlane's claim was rejected.

This case relates to both grounds of appeal. In relation to the first ground of appeal, for example, the Appellant may use this case to support an argument that Andrew was a mere bystander and would not be able to recover as a secondary victim in the circumstances.

In relation to the second ground of appeal, the Respondent and Appellant may use this case to respectively argue that Andrew did or did not have proximity on the basis that his injuries were or were not reasonably foreseeable in the circumstances.

Galli-Atkinson v Seghal [2003] EWCA Civ. 697

Presiding Court This case was heard in the Court of Appeal (Civil Division).

Synopsis The claimant's 16-year-old daughter was killed following a car crash. The claimant arrived after her daughter was removed from the scene and she only saw her body in the mortuary. The body was badly disfigured. It was established that the claimant had viewed the body during the 'immediate aftermath' of the incident. The incident in this case occurred at 7.05pm. The Court of Appeal found that the claimant was present at two stages within the 'immediate aftermath' of the accident, namely at 8.20pm when she arrived at the scene, and at 9.20pm when she saw her daughter's body in the mortuary.

Relevance to the Grounds of Appeal This case relates to the second ground of appeal in that it focuses upon the concept of proximity, and how long of a time period could be considered to form part of the 'immediate aftermath' of an incident. In relation to Andrew, this case has some factual parallels to his experience of seeing James on the video call, at the scene and at the hospital. The court's decision therefore might inform whether the different stages in his perception of James amounted to him being present in the 'immediate aftermath' of the incident. Of course, given the phrasing of the second ground of appeal, the video call is the crucial event here.

Again, the closeness of the relationship between the primary and secondary victim in *Galli-Atkinson* was not at issue.

Taylor v A Novo (UK) Ltd [2013] EWCA Civ. 194

Presiding Court   This case was heard in the Court of Appeal (Civil Division).

Synopsis   In *Taylor* the claimant's mother was injured at work when, through the negligence of a fellow employee, a stack of racking boards fell on top of her. She had apparently made a recovery, but three weeks later she suddenly died at home. The claimant did not witness the accident at the store, but did witness her mother's death. She suffered post-traumatic stress disorder as a consequence. She pursued a claim for damages against her mother's former employer. The claimant's case in the Court of Appeal re-visited *Alcock*. She argued that the courts had taken a less strict approach to relevant claims in the two decades since *Alcock*, in terms of proximity, and she therefore qualified as a secondary victim.

The Court of Appeal rejected the argument and found that the existing limitations on qualification should apply unless Parliament intervened.

Relevance to the Grounds of Appeal   This case is relevant to the second ground of appeal. This case considers the question of proximity in terms of liability for a secondary victim who was not present at the scene of an accident. The Court of Appeal distinguished *Taylor* from *Galli-Atkinson v Seghal* on the basis that, in that case, there was a 'seamless tale of events' and 'one drawn out experience'. *Taylor*, the court said, was 'certainly *not* part of a single event or seamless tale'.

In relation to Andrew, this means that he, i.e. the Respondent, will likely need to argue that the different stages he encountered (i.e. the video call, witnessing the scene and bedside vigil) all amounted to a 'seamless sequence of events'.

Again, the closeness of the relationship between the primary and secondary victim in *Taylor* was not at issue.

Shorter v Surrey and Sussex Healthcare NHS Trust [2015] EWHC 614 QB

Presiding Court
This case was heard in the Queen's Bench Division. The QBD is one of the three divisions of the High Court of Justice, together with the Chancery Division and the Family Division. It is bound by the decisions of higher courts. The QBD handles negligence cases routinely.

Synopsis
The claimant's sister had collapsed with a severe headache and was admitted to hospital. A CT scan was performed and she was told that she had not suffered a subarachnoid haemorrhage. She was discharged, but later re-admitted with pain, and a review of the CT scan showed that she had suffered a haemorrhage a week earlier. The sister's husband telephoned the claimant to inform her that there had been an undetected haemorrhage, and that her sister's condition had worsened. The claimant was a senior sister (nurse) in a neuro-intensive care unit and was aware of the seriousness of her sister's condition and the possibility of a further haemorrhage. She attended the hospital and claimed that she saw her sister rolling around on a trolley, crying with pain, clutching her head and saying that she was in agony. She received a call later at home informing her that her sister had suffered a seizure, and then later another call to say that she had started fitting. She attended the hospital and saw her sister on life support and was told by the sister's husband that she had 'gone'. The sister had died. The claimant suffered from a major depressive disorder and sought damages from the Trust.

The court dismissed the claim. The court found that the incidents over the two days of the second hospital admission had contributed to the claimant's injury; however, she also had to show that her psychiatric illness had been caused by the sight or sound causing an assault on her senses.

Relevance to the Grounds of Appeal

In relation to the first ground of appeal, it is noteworthy that this case related to siblings, which is a relationship that *Alcock* did not consider to automatically qualify as a relationship of sufficiently close ties of love and affection. In *Shorter*, the court implicitly accepted that the siblings had a relationship of 'sufficiently close ties of love and affection'. Thus, *Shorter* arguably represents a widening of *Alcock* in this context. Although, a mooter should look at the distinct circumstances explained in *Shorter* for this being so. In *Shorter*, the court made it clear that these particular sisters shared a relationship akin to mother and daughter, as such it may not be a material widening at all. Still, the Respondent could use this case to bolster the argument that a wider interpretation of *Alcock* is now permissible.

In relation to the second ground of appeal, the *Shorter* court commented that there had not been a seamless single horrifying event, as the most horrifying news had been relayed to the claimant by telephone, or by face-to-face conversations with her brother-in-law. In other words, the claimant had not directly perceived them herself. Even when she had witnessed her sister on the life support machine, her perception had been informed by the information she had been receiving over the previous 15 hours and by her own professional knowledge. In relation to Andrew, *Shorter* informs the Appellant and Respondent position on whether Andrew's experience was part of a seamless chain of events, and also whether his communication with James via video call was sufficient in terms of proximity. *Shorter* suggests that a telephone call, on these facts, is insufficient. As such, it may be helpful to the Appellant. However, of course, both Junior Counsel will be aware that Andrew's experience was slightly different to that in *Shorter*, in that his telephone call involved a (albeit broken) video stream.

These summaries show how the case law has progressed and how the law in this area is quite nuanced in terms of who qualifies as a secondary victim.

It is also important to note that, in addition to her cases, Anna made use of a journal article. Although scholarship is not binding on any court, if relevant, it may be persuasive. Anna chose an article titled 'Donal Nolan, *Horrifying events and their consequences: clarifying the operation of the Alcock criteria*, (2014) 30(3) PN 176'. This article provides commentary on some of the case law mentioned above, and therefore might be useful for mooters in formulating interpretations of the case holdings.

SUMMARY

As you will have seen from this chapter, approaches to research can differ between individuals and between moot problems. Despite the different approaches taken by Ali and Anna, both manage to find appropriate case law and principles in this area. The aim of this section is to provide you with a toolkit that will enable you to get started with legal research. This moot problem should have highlighted to you the importance of precision in your legal research, given the majority of the law in this area has evolved incrementally and subtly in different cases.

While this problem, like the criminal law problem, may have also been about the development of the common law, there are some important distinctions that you should have understood at this stage. In particular, the criminal law problem question was concerned with: (1) how the terms of an established legislative provision, namely s1(1) Criminal Attempts Act 1981 were to be interpreted in different cases; and (2) how an established principle of law, i.e. that duress is not a defence to attempted murder, applied (if at all) in certain circumstances.

In **Live and Loud Ltd v Hacker-Jones**, however, both grounds of appeal are concerned with case law that presented a nuanced development of phrases when it comes to determining secondary victims in this context. This nuanced development necessitates good research that sufficiently engages in the detail of the case law concerned. This is only something, however, that would be understood once you have sufficiently engaged in your research. The key test for whether you are able to begin constructing your argument will always be whether you feel confident that you know the key legal tests and are assured that they are the most up-to-date principles. You may need to return to research later, but if you have the confidence that you know the key areas, then you are ready to begin the next part of your preparation: constructing your argument.

ARGUMENT CONSTRUCTION

Once you have selected your authorities, you need to think about how to use them to support your overarching argument. This is the point where, if you have not yet done so, you need to begin to consider your argument from the particular position that you have been allocated, be it Appellant or Respondent. Once you begin to consider authorities in this directed fashion, you are able to start constructing your skeleton argument.

PRELIMINARY CONSIDERATIONS FOR CONSTRUCTING A SKELETON ARGUMENT

Remember the three main areas that we identified in the criminal law chapter for consideration when constructing your skeleton argument on page 29. These, in brief, are:

- **Your overarching argument.** You must be clear on what your overall argument is.
- **Submissions.** You should aim for three key arguments.
- **Drafting.** Your skeleton will require careful editing to ensure it is professional, clear and concise.

You should also make sure that you remember the other considerations that were identified earlier as significant when drafting a skeleton argument:

- **What do you want?** Focus on your overall point.
- **Brevity.** Ensure you draft and redraft your work.
- **Best foot forward.** Start with your strongest point.
- **Is the law on your side?** Know the law!
- **Terminology.** Be clear on any particular phrases or technical ideas.
- **Anticipate.** Think about the arguments of the other side and the position of the judge.
- **Authorities and purpose.** Position your authorities carefully and be clear on why you are using them.

SUBMISSIONS FOR THE APPELLANT

We will first of all consider how Ali and Anna developed submissions for the Appellant.

Senior Appellant

The ground of appeal that Ali was working on was:

> Andrew did not have a sufficiently close tie of 'love and affection' with James at the time of the incident and therefore does not qualify as a secondary victim. *Alcock v Chief Constable of South Yorkshire* [1992] 1 AC 310.

As the Appellant, Ali's overarching argument would be:

> Andrew *did not* have sufficiently close ties of 'love and affection' with James at the time of the incident and therefore *does not* qualify as a secondary victim.

From Ali's analysis of both the problem question and the ground of appeal, and his research, Ali determined that he needed to address the following 'points':

> 1. The civil partnership between Andrew and James gives rise to a presumption of close ties of love and affection. This may be rebutted by the separation of the couple and the questions surrounding Andrew's infidelity. However, Andrew's action's after the fire may counter these facts.
>
> 2. If there is no 'close tie of love and affection' between Andrew and James, the Respondent would become a mere bystander, if he fulfils the proximity requirements. *McFarlane* found that bystanders cannot claim as secondary victims in nervous shock cases, absent foreseeable consequences. Note *McFarlane* could be distinguished from the instant case.

Ali began by developing points that were inclined towards the Appellant, but that also acknowledged possible courses of action by the Respondent. This stands him in good stead, not only in terms of developing his argument for the Appellant, but also in terms of preparing to respond to the other side.

Subsequently, Ali used these points to flesh out three submissions. He followed our general advice, developing three initial submissions as Senior Appellant, which can be seen below:

---

1. The presumption of close ties of love and affection can be rebutted. *Alcock* and *Shorter* can be used to support this argument.

2. The Respondent became a mere bystander and therefore cannot claim as a secondary victim. *McFarlane* can be used to support this point.

3. Policy argument discussing the creation of a new line of precedent based on the special circumstances of the relationship in the present case and how it broke down.

Ali followed an appropriate structure by focusing upon the key test that forms the basis of his ground of review. He utilises his two legal submissions to argue, first, that the test is not satisfied and that, second, this leaves Andrew in no position to claim. He also seeks to develop a policy submission to argue against any possible change or development of the law.

Following these early ideas for submissions, Ali then redrafted them into the following form:

---

1. The Respondent did not share a close relationship of love and affection with the primary victim at the time of the incident which caused his death. (*Alcock v Chief Constable of South Yorkshire* [1992] 1 AC 310, *Shorter v Surrey and Sussex Healthcare NHS Trust* [2015] EWHC 614). The presumption in favour of the Respondent can be rebutted by the fact that rumours of his infidelity had been circulating among their friends, and the fact that he was on a date at the time of the primary victim's accident.

2. The Respondent fails to meet the relevant criteria for a special relationship because he was a mere bystander who was on the scene at the time of the incident (*McFarlane v EE Caledonia Ltd* [1994] 2 All ER 1). The claim will fail because, in the absence of a close tie of love and affection between the primary and secondary victims, the Respondent would fall into the category of bystander as seen in McFarlane.

3. Alcock and Shorter are distinguishable because the present case concerns a relationship which has broken down and an accident which occurred when the relationship was far from affectionate. As there is no case law to assist the court in this area, this is a perfect opportunity to preclude psychiatric injury claims where love and affection existed in the past but not at the time of the actual event in question.

These submissions begin to give more depth to Ali's key arguments, but careful editing injects further clarity into them. Below we provide edited versions of Ali's submissions and explain why we made the amendments:

1. The Respondent did not share a 'close relationship of love and affection' with the primary victim at the time of the incident that caused his death. Any presumption in favour of the Respondent, due to the existence of his civil partnership with the primary victim, can be rebutted by the circumstances surrounding their separation. See *Alcock v Chief Constable of South Yorkshire* **[1992] 1 AC 310**; and *Shorter v Surrey and Sussex Healthcare NHS Trust* [2015] EWHC 614.

Our edits focus on improving Ali's drafting with regards to the second sentence of his submission. We have removed specific facts about their relationship and replaced them with more general wording. This approach provides Ali with some flexibility, but also puts across his central point, i.e. that the close ties of love and affection between the Respondent and primary victim had broken down at the time of the incident.

2. In failing to meet the requirement of 'close tie of love and affection', the Respondent falls into the category of a 'mere bystander'. Therefore, following the decision of this Court in *McFarlane v EE Caledonia Ltd* **[1994] 2 All ER 1**, the Respondent is unable to claim as a secondary victim.

Our edits seek to engender a closer connection between submission one and submission two, as they are inextricably linked. It also informs the instant court how the Appellant wishes it to 'use' the McFarlane case. This adds clarity to the submission.

3. This Court should maintain the courts' conservative approach towards defining secondary victims, as initiated in *Alcock* and confirmed more recently in *Shorter*. This approach should be continued in situations, like that of the instant case, where close ties of love and affection previously existed, but were absent at the time of the relevant event.

Our edits aim to formalise Ali's language, and clarify for the court how he wishes to 'use' the Alcock and Shorter cases.

Junior Appellant

The ground of appeal that Anna was working on was:

> **The lower court had placed too broad an interpretation on the dicta from** *Alcock*. **Andrew was not sufficiently proximate to the incident via the video call.**

Acting for the Appellant, Anna's overarching argument is:

> **The lower court** *did* **place too broad an interpretation on the dicta from Alcock. Andrew** *was not* **sufficiently proximate to the incident via the video call.**

Anna developed the following 'points' as being central to her ground:

- Was the interpretation too broad?

- How broad can the interpretation be when applying the Alcock test?

- Does the video call amount to lack of proximity like watching events on television?

- Is there an exception on proximity with video calls when the parties are in a close relationship?

- Does the video call amount to proximity to the event without considering the immediate aftermath?

- The respondent was proximate to the immediate aftermath and should therefore not consider the video call.

- Is the law going to change due to the evolution of the technological means of communication? If yes, then a video call can amount to sufficient proximity.

Anna also took quite a neutral and broad approach in the number and type of points that she developed. At this early stage, Anna began to incorporate legal concepts, which shows a different method compared to her very fact-heavy approach to the criminal law problem question at this stage. This is a positive development for Anna, as ground two of the appeal is very precise and it would be difficult for her to be considering the facts in a manner entirely divorced from the law.

Following these broad points, Anna ordered and consolidated them in to three submissions. These were as follows:

1. The interpretation was too broad and does not meet the criteria of the *Alcock* test. ***Alcock v Chief Constable of South Yorkshire***.

2. Andrew was not sufficiently proximate to the accident via the video call and it is too unforeseeable. ***McFarlane v EE Caledonia***.

3. To disallow this appeal will lead to a massive amount of unsupported claims and open the floodgates. **Horrifying events and their consequences: clarifying the Alcock criteria**.

Anna has sought to develop three submissions that cover all parts of the ground of appeal and has phrased them in a relatively informal way at this stage. She has, however, already included a 'key' authority for each of her submissions, which will again help her in further developing them for her skeleton argument. Anna, like Ali, sought to focus upon the particular test that her ground of review revolves around, namely that of proximity. Notably, she chooses to focus on the issue of foreseeability of harm, as opposed to the concept of 'immediate aftermath'. This is something that the judge and opposing counsel might pick up on, as we see later on in the Respondent's skeleton argument on pages 80–81 and in considering potential judicial questions on page 83.

Following this early attempt, Anna redrafted her submissions into the following:

1. The interpretation by the lower courts on the *Alcock* dicta was too broad and evidently the defendant does not meet the criteria arising from the case of ***Alcock v Chief Constable of South Yorkshire*** **[1992] 1 AC 310.**

2. Being proximate through a video call was not a foreseeable cause of psychological harm and the defendant cannot claim following the case of ***McFarlane v Wilkinson*** **[1997] 2 Lloyd's Rep. 259.**

3. Disallowing this appeal will open the floodgates and will allow future claimants to claim with no basis, which might also lead to a change of the law. **Donal Nolan, *Horrifying events and their consequences: clarifying the operation of the Alcock criteria*.**

Anna has begun to develop her points into clearer and more distinct submissions for her ground of appeal. These initial drafts can also be improved by careful editing. Below we provide edited versions of Anna's submissions, with explanations for our edits:

1. The lower court's interpretation of *Alcock v Chief Constable of South Yorkshire* **[1992] 1 AC 310** was too broad. As stated by the House of Lords in *Alcock*, the viewing of a traumatic event through the transmission of live, electronic images is insufficient for the purposes of proximity. This Court should follow the House of Lords' approach and find that the video call did not place the Respondent sufficiently proximate to the event. As such, the Respondent does not qualify as a secondary victim.

Our edits aim to clarify Anna's use of Alcock in relation to the instant case facts. It does this by focusing on Alcock's interpretation of television images and drawing a parallel to the video call.

2. The psychological harm suffered by the Respondent was not a foreseeable consequence of the video call, as per this Court in *McFarlane v EE Caledonia Ltd* **[1994] 2 All ER 1.** The Respondent therefore does not qualify as a secondary victim.

Again, our edits seek to clarify Anna's argument and indicate how she plans to 'use' the McFarlane case.

3. The Court should continue the courts' cautious approach towards defining proximity. See: *Alcock*. Rejecting this appeal will place too broad an interpretation on *Alcock*. Widening the concept of proximity to include video calls would dangerously widen the concept of proximity given the constant advancement of communication technology. See **Donal Nolan, *Horrifying events and their consequences: clarifying the operation of the Alcock criteria,* (2014) 30(3) PN 176.**

Our edits seek to clarify Anna's argument, formalise her language and improve her sentence construction. We also provide a fuller citation for her selected journal article. The edits also narrow Anna's floodgates argument by putting it into context, i.e. relating it to the advancement of technological communication. This is an important point, as generalising too widely tends to provide a judge with an immediate concern about your argument and, thus, is not very persuasive. Anna's core point is that if the court agrees that the video call is sufficient to satisfy proximity, then this widening of proximity threatens to be never-ending. This is because new technology is constantly being developed, and rejecting the appeal would effectively create a precedent that compels courts to find that communication through these various means is sufficiently proximate for the purposes of identifying secondary victims in this context. This would be a major departure from the Alcock precedent.

You should contrast the edited submissions against Ali and Anna's draft submissions carefully. The general themes across our edits are that we have sought to clarify their arguments, increase the formality of their drafting and indicate more clearly how they plan to interpret the case law they cite. This approach can be seen in the example Respondent skeleton argument we drafted on the next page.

IN THE COURT OF APPEAL (CIVIL DIVISION)

Live and Loud Ltd v. Jones-Hacker

Respondent's Skeleton Argument

Senior Counsel for the Respondent shall submit:

Ground One:

1. As demonstrated by their conduct during and after the fire, the Respondent and primary victim shared sufficiently 'close ties of love and affection' at the time of the incident. Such relationships are not confined to traditional relationships. See *Shorter v Surrey and Sussex Healthcare NHS Trust* **[2015] EWHC 614**. Therefore, applying the reasoning of the House of Lords in *Alcock v Chief Constable of South Yorkshire* **[1992] 1 AC 310** the Respondent qualifies as a secondary victim.

2. If the Respondent was a 'mere bystander', his injuries were reasonably foreseeable, unlike in the case of *McFarlane v EE Caledonia Ltd* **[1994] 2 All ER 1**.

3. The Court should continue the pragmatic approach taken by the courts towards determining what relationships comprise 'close ties of love and affection'. *See, Alcock* and *Shorter*. Rejecting this appeal will not disturb that approach, but allow a legal remedy solely in cases that reflect the narrow facts of the instant case. A decision finding that a brief separation between spouses extinguishes close ties of love and affection would be improper and unrealistic.

Junior Counsel for the Respondent shall submit:

Ground Two:

1. The Respondent was sufficiently proximate to the event and its 'immediate aftermath' in order to qualify as a secondary victim. When considering the video call, together with the Respondent's presence at the scene and bedside vigil, there was a single 'seamless stream of events' that gives rise to sufficient proximity. *See, Galli-Atkinson v Seghal* **[2003] EWCA Civ. 697**; and *Taylor v A Novo (UK) Ltd* **[2013] EWCA Civ. 194**.

2. The Respondent's contact with the primary victim via video call gives rise to sufficient proximity. This is because technology enabled him to perceive the fire visually and with audio. This Court should follow its decision in *Galli-Atkinson* and find the Respondent was sufficiently proximate to be a secondary victim.

3. The Respondent urges this Court to revisit the approach taken by the House of Lords in *Alcock*, with regards to proximity, in light of modern technology and communication methods. The House of Lords' assessment in *Alcock* concerning images broadcast from televisions in the early 1990s is wholly distinguishable. Allowing a video call to render secondary victims as sufficiently proximate to an event (in cases such as the instant) would be reasonable in light of the quality and intimate nature of such technology.

The Respondent respectfully requests that this appeal be dismissed.

Senior Counsel: Dr Scarlett McArdle **Junior Counsel:** Dr Sarah Cooper

THINKING AHEAD AND BEING CRITICAL

Once your submissions are drafted, you must start to think critically about your argument. This involves thinking ahead to what sorts of questions the judge might ask you during the course of your moot. The two concepts are closely related because the judge will seek to clarify and test your arguments by asking questions that address the weaknesses in your arguments.

We will now advance our consideration of judicial questioning from the approach taken in the criminal law chapter, which merely introduced you to the types of questions you might get asked in relation to each ground of appeal. In this chapter (using Ali and Anna's edited submissions for the Appellant), we provide examples of submission-specific questions and examples of questions related to the relevant law topic in general. In the contract law and human rights law chapters we will advance our approach further by providing examples of responses you could give to specific questions. For now, however, you must simply get familiar with the phrasing and nature of judicial questioning.

Submission-Specific Questions

Ground One

1. The Respondent did not share a 'close relationship of love and affection' with the primary victim at the time of the incident which caused his death. Any presumption in favour of the Respondent, due to the existence of his civil partnership with the primary victim, can be rebutted by the circumstances surrounding their separation. See *Alcock v Chief Constable of South Yorkshire* [1992] 1 AC 310; and *Shorter v Surrey and Sussex Healthcare NHS Trust* [2015] EWHC 614.

   - *What specific circumstances, around the relationship of the Respondent and primary victim, do you say rebut the presumption that they shared a relationship of 'close ties of love and affection'?*
   - *Shorter provides an example of a court impliedly widening the type of relationship that can share a close tie of love and affection for the purposes of identifying a secondary victim in this context. Should this Court not follow that approach?*

2. In failing to meet the requirement of 'close tie of love and affection', the Respondent falls into the category of a 'mere bystander'. Therefore, following the decision of this Court in *McFarlane v EE Caledonia Ltd* [1994] 2 All ER 1, the Respondent is unable to claim as a secondary victim.

   - *Is McFarlane not wholly distinguishable from the instant case on its facts?*
   - *If, theoretically, this court rejects your first submission, is this second submission irrelevant?*

3. This Court should maintain the courts' conservative approach towards defining secondary victims, as initiated in *Alcock* and confirmed most recently in *Shorter*. This approach should be continued in situations, like that of the instant case, where close ties of love and affection previously existed, but were absent at the time of the relevant event.

   - *How do the cases of Alcock and Shorter represent a conservative approach? Can you identify specific passages in both cases to support this argument?*
   - *Would it be unrealistic to hold that a married couple, merely separated for a few weeks, did not share 'close ties of love and affection'?*

Ground Two

1. The lower court's interpretation of *Alcock v Chief Constable of South York-shire* [1992] 1 AC 310 was too broad. As stated by the House of Lords in *Alcock*, the viewing of a traumatic event through the transmission of live, electronic images is insufficient for the purposes of proximity. This Court should follow the House of Lords' approach and find that the video call did not place the Respondent sufficiently proximate to the event. As such, the Respondent does not qualify as a secondary victim.

   - *Do you seek to draw a parallel between the television images broadcast in Alcock and the video call in the instant case? If so, are these two modes of communication not significantly different?*
   - *Is this Court bound by the House of Lord's decision in Alcock on this precise point?*

2. The psychological harm suffered by the Respondent was not a foreseeable consequence of the video call, as per this Court in *McFarlane v EE Caledonia Ltd* [1994] 2 All ER 1. The Respondent therefore does not qualify as a second-ary victim.

   - *Is McFarlane applicable to the instant case? Should you not be addressing the issues of proximity as raised in cases such as Galli-Atkinson v Seghal [2003] EWCA Civ. 697, for example?*
   - *If this is an issue of foreseeability, is it not conceivable that such harm was reasonably foreseeable? After all, the Respondent witnessed the primary victim in the fire through a live, direct image?*

3. The Court should continue the courts' cautious approach towards defining proximity. See: *Alcock*. Rejecting this appeal will place too broad an interpre-tation on *Alcock*. Widening the concept of proximity to include video calls would dangerously widen the concept of proximity given the constant advancement of communication technology. See Donal Nolan, *Horrifying events and their consequences: clarifying the operation of the Alcock criteria*, (2014) 30(3) PN 176.

   - *Is the Appellant being too pessimistic about the potential for a decision in favour of the Respondent to cause a floodgate situation? Can a decision in favour of the Respondent not be confined to the specific facts of this case?*
   - *The law must, to an appropriate extent, reflect societal changes. In order to reflect societal change with regards to the use of technology, should this court not feel compelled to find that the video call did place the Respondent sufficiently proximate to the event?*

General Topic Area (and Curve Ball) Questions

It is also important to consider what general questions a judge may ask you, which are not specific to your submissions, but may relate to the law in general or, indeed, be curve balls. Below are some examples of such questions, which a judge might ask any (and all) of the advocates mooting in the case of **Live and Loud Ltd v Andrew Jones-Hacker**.

- *Could you clarify all of the tests that must be satisfied in order for a person to be determined a secondary victim in this context?*

- *Are you familiar with the Law Commission's report 'Liability for Psychiatric Illness, Law Com. 249 (1998)'? If so, what observations do you have about its content as it relates to your ground of appeal?*

- *Was the House of Lords' decision in Alcock unanimous?*

- *How are the two grounds of this appeal linked? Is one dependent on the other?*

It is important to anticipate these sorts of questions, which underscore the need to prepare widely and engross yourself in the general subject area. Sometimes a judge may ask a question that you do not know the answer to when engaging in this sort of generalised questioning. Chapter 6 will suggest ways that you can address such questions appropriately.

SUMMARY

Constructing a clear and logical argument that addresses the grounds of appeal in a comprehensive way, which accounts for both their strengths and weaknesses, is vital to preparing to moot successfully.

It is also important to remember that the construction of your skeleton argument and your critical assessment of it is just one step (albeit a significant one) in preparing to moot. Once you have completed this process, it is time to develop your extended oral presentation. We provide some guidance on how to do this in the final chapter of the book.

CONCLUSION

In this chapter, we have shown you how to analyse, research and construct an argument in relation to the moot problem presented by the fictitious case of **Live and Loud Ltd v Andrew Jones-Hacker**.

3

HUMAN RIGHTS LAW

INTRODUCTION

In this chapter, we will show you how to analyse, research and construct an argument in relation to the moot problem presented by the fictitious case of **Swifter and Handsworth v Daily Herald**. This is a human rights law themed moot problem question.

This first section will focus on analysing the moot problem. We will begin by deconstructing the problem question and introduce you to its basic, but fundamental, features. Next, we will focus on summarising the problem question. We will then consider how to interpret the grounds of appeal and the angle you should take for your allocated role. Finally, we will examine how to derive search terms from a problem question, to allow you to progress on to researching the relevant area of law.

In this question, Ali and Anna undertook the roles of Senior Appellant and Senior Respondent respectively, and we crafted arguments for the Junior Appellant and Junior Respondent.

ANALYSIS

THE PROBLEM QUESTION

A **IN THE SUPREME COURT OF THE UNITED KINGDOM**

SWIFTER AND HANDSWORTH **B**

V

DAILY HERALD **C**

D Milly Swifter is a young pop star who recently got married to the children's television presenter Laurence Handsworth. Milly is particularly known for her sexually provocative songs and dance routines. Laurence, on the other hand, has a particularly clean-cut image. To try and maintain this, both were keen for the wedding and marriage to be a private affair. There was a great deal of secrecy about the wedding due to concern at the disapproval of the relationship from Laurence's friends, family and co-workers.

Milly's ex-boyfriend, Paddy Schwarz, was particularly outraged by the marriage and decided to sell the story of his relationship with Milly to the newspapers, one of which was the Daily Herald. This gave huge detail of their lurid sex life and explained that the breakdown of their relationship had arisen out of Milly's increasing drug use and her infidelity with Laurence. The Daily Herald printed this story, alongside details and photos of the wedding. These photos included images from the wedding party showing Milly and Laurence intoxicated and using drugs. One of the images, in particular, showed Laurence in the presence of a group of teenage girls, while taking cocaine and smoking cannabis. All of the images concerned, as well as the stories, have since been picked up and reproduced by news websites and social media.

E Milly Swifter and Laurence Handsworth brought proceedings in the High Court for infringement of the right to respect for privacy, relying on *Douglas v Hello! Ltd (No. 1)* [2001] 2 All ER 289 and *Campbell v Mirror Group Newspapers Ltd* [2004] UKHL 22.

At the trial, Douglas J found:

F 1. There was no reasonable expectation of privacy with regard to their wedding, its details and the details of their relationship due to the manner in which Milly Swifter and Laurence Handsworth courted the press.

2. Any right to respect for privacy was outweighed by the public interest in the photos being published, in particular the images of drug use around young fans.

The Court of Appeal unanimously upheld the judgment of Douglas J. Swifter and Handsworth now appeal to the Supreme Court.

G 1. Both Milly Swifter and Laurence Handsworth had a reasonable expectation of privacy, regarding their relationship, their wedding and the photographs taken at their wedding.

H 2. The right to respect for privacy was not outweighed by any public interest in the publication of the story or photographs surrounding Laurence's drug use.

UNDERSTANDING THE BASICS OF THE PROBLEM QUESTION

Again we will begin by analysing the moot problem question. Below you will find a list of features identified by the relevant letter in the problem question above.

A **COURT**
Swifter and Handsworth v Daily Herald is being heard in the UK Supreme Court. You should refresh yourself and take note of what this means in terms of precedent and the decisions this court can take.

B **APPELLANT**
The first name indicates who is appealing to the appeal court. The Appellants in this case are Milly Swifter and Laurence Handsworth. The fact that there are two Appellants in the instant case should not change your overall approach, as they are both making the same claims.

C **RESPONDENT**
The second name indicates who is responding to the appeal. In this case, the Daily Herald is the Respondent. The Daily Herald is a company (as opposed to a private individual) but this should not change the arguments made by counsel on either side.

D **INCIDENT FACTS**
These paragraphs outline the initial facts of the case, including details of the relationship between the Appellants. The wedding between the two Appellants is integral to both grounds of an appeal. In sum, the Appellants are arguing that they had a right to privacy during their wedding. The grounds of appeal make two cumulative arguments about this. See letters 'G' and 'H' for an explanation.

E **CLAIM**

This explains the initial claim that Milly Swifter and Laurence Handsworth made against the Daily Herald.

F **IMMEDIATE PROCEDURAL HISTORY**

This tells you what has happened in the court directly below the court in which the moot problem question is in.

G **GROUND ONE OF THE APPEAL**

This ground 'belongs' to Senior Counsel for both the Appellant and the Respondent. The Appellant will argue for the appeal, whereas the Respondent will argue against. This is the first of two cumulative arguments. Senior Counsel for the Appellants must argue that the Appellants had a 'reasonable expectation of privacy' at their wedding. Only if this argument succeeds does ground two become relevant.

H **GROUND TWO OF THE APPEAL**

This ground 'belongs' to Junior Counsel for both the Appellant and Respondent. This ground is only relevant if the Appellants are successful with regards to ground one. There would only be a consideration as to whether there would be an overriding public interest in disclosing the relevant information about the wedding, if the Appellants had a reasonable expectation of privacy in the first place.

SUMMARISING THE CASE

We will now summarise the moot question in preparation for analysing the problem in more detail. This sub-section will begin with the summaries constructed by Ali and Anna. These summaries will form the basis for constructing a summary that is simultaneously concise and comprehensive.

Below is the summary constructed by Ali:

- *Milly Swifter, a pop star, married Laurence Handsworth, a children's TV presenter. Laurence's image had previously always been clean but Milly was well known for her sexually provocative songs and dance routines. They wished to keep the wedding quiet to maintain Laurence's image.*

- *Paddy Schwarz, Milly's ex-boyfriend, contacted the Daily Herald and sold them stories and pictures of his sex life with Milly to gain revenge for Milly's infidelity with Laurence. The Daily Herald also published pictures of the wedding, which contained damning evidence of both Milly and Laurence using drugs.*

> • MS and LH brought a claim in the high court to suppress the story which they believed infringed their right to respect for their privacy. Their claim was dismissed, and the Court of Appeal dismissed their appeal. They now appeal to the Supreme Court on the grounds that their right to respect to privacy had been infringed, and that this was not outweighed by any issues of public interest.

Ali deviates from the general rule of a five-point summary. Ali is seeking to phrase the summary in his own words rather than lifting text from the problem question. This shows a good approach; if you are able to phrase a summary in your own words, then you will generally understand the fact pattern well enough to present a summary well. However, paraphrasing should always be done cautiously. The drafter should be mindful of not losing clarity of meaning, especially with the grounds of appeal. Ali's summary suffers from this. His articulation of the current appeal does not encapsulate the bespoke language of the appeal. Our summary shows to integrate such language concisely. That said, Ali has logically ordered his points. They follow the problem chronologically and include the key facts. Ali could be 'punchier' in his summarising and you will see our example of this below.

Below is the summary constructed by Anna:

> Milly Swifter and Laurence Handsworth are both celebrities. Milly is a pop star and Laurence works for kids programmes. They got married under strictly private circumstances to avoid disapproval by Laurence's friends and family. However, Milly's ex, Paddy Schwarz, decided to give away to the press information about Milly's life and pictures of the wedding. They are now bringing proceedings for infringement of their right to respect for their privacy. The Court of Appeal upheld the judgment and they are now appealing to the Supreme Court.

Anna shows consistency in her approach to summarising; she again provides prose rather than points. While Anna does include key points in her summary, she is sometimes a little too brief (for example, when she articulates the current grounds of appeal) and the language that she uses is sometimes a bit too informal (for example, her use of the terms 'kids' and 'give away').

Below is an example of a summary we developed to try and take a middle ground between Ali and Anna's approaches.

- *Milly Swifter and Laurence Handsworth are celebrities who recently married in a secret wedding ceremony.*

- *The wedding was held in secret due to concerns about Swifter's sexualised image and its impact on Handsworth's career in children's television.*

- *Controversial photographs and details were leaked to the press and published extensively.*

- *Swifter and Handsworth made a claim against the Daily Herald for breach of privacy, which was rejected at first instance and in the Court of Appeal.*

- *They now appeal to the Supreme Court on the basis that they had a reasonable expectation of privacy and that there was no overriding public interest in the information published to override this right.*

We have followed our general guidance of including key facts and excluding extraneous detail. When constructing the summary, it was important to include details as to the relationships in the problem but also the specific issues surrounding the allegations of a breach of privacy, namely, the information and pictures disclosed to the press. It was also still important to reference the history of the case and the current appeal points before the Supreme Court. In particular, we have remained close to the wording of the grounds of appeal. This is because they are specific, in the sense that they are not concerned with a general right to respect for privacy, but rather more tailored legal tests associated with that right. The above summary encompasses all of these key points.

Now you have reviewed three attempts at summarising a moot problem question, you should be clear that a good summary encompasses three characteristics:

1. **Provides a useful balance between being sufficiently concise yet inclusive of key facts**. You will see from Ali and Anna's various summaries that this is a difficult balance to achieve. The best way to ensure this balance is to carry out multiple edits of your summary.
2. **Uses appropriate language that is sufficiently formal and provides clarity of meaning**. These are two different things. You should be mindful not to use informal language or slang in a moot, given the formal nature of legal argument before courts. Clarity is required because of the very complexity of law. A slight lack of clarity in a legal argument can have a significant impact on both the accuracy and the meaning of a legal

argument. Legal frameworks are drafted in a particular way for a reason; each term has been carefully selected. Mooters and lawyers must appreciate this and construct arguments appropriately.

3. **Employs a logical structure**. Presenting a summary in a logical order helps the drafter to achieve characteristics 1 and 2 above. As shown, approaching the summary in a chronological order is often the best way to approach this.

From Ali and Anna's three attempts at summarising, it is evident that characteristics 1 and 2 are often difficult for students to achieve. Practice is the only way to resolve this issue. With that in mind, below is a short story that you can use to undertake further practice at summarising. You should read the story and attempt a five-point summary.

Cynthia is a retired nurse. At the age of 45, she was diagnosed with MS, cancer of the bowel and diabetes. Despite this being a very upsetting diagnosis, Cynthia's cancer was caught early and could be operated on, and her diabetes could be easily controlled by medication. Cynthia's doctors' main concern was her MS and the extent to which this condition would shorten her life expectancy. By the age of 50, Cynthia's MS had progressed significantly and she required daily care. Cynthia's daughter, Patsy, arranged for Cynthia to move into a care home, where she could be attended to properly. This was arranged through Poplar District Council. However, due to budget cuts there were no rooms available in council ran homes, so Cynthia was housed in a private care home, Buckle Care Home. After a few months of living at the care home, Patsy noticed when visiting her mother that she was often hungry and dehydrated. Patsy made her concerns known to the care home manager, Julian, but felt that her comments were dismissed. Weeks later, Cynthia was rushed to hospital. The hospital staff quickly realised that Cynthia was not being fed sufficiently and was suffering from malnutrition and dehydration. She also had bedsores from not being moved frequently. Patsy was enraged. Patsy brought a claim against Buckle Care Home on the basis that her mother had been subjected to inhumane and degrading treatment, in violation of Article 3 of the European Convention of Human Rights as incorporated into English law through section 2 of the Human Rights Act 1998. The claim is currently being heard at first instance.

UNDERSTANDING YOUR GROUND OF APPEAL

In a human rights problem, it is important to be specific about which right(s) are being questioned before the court. In the same way as in the other problem questions, it is important to show an understanding of the focus of the appeal points. As a starting point, you need to be clear on the legal frameworks in existence here and how the applicable rights have become legally enforceable in English law. Below we will give a short explanation of this area. You will need to do more detailed reading to fully understand this, but this short introduction should help guide you through the chapter and introduce you to some essentials.

In the United Kingdom, the starting point for human rights will be the European Convention on Human Rights, as incorporated into UK law through the Human Rights Act 1998. This distinction of an international treaty being incorporated into domestic law by a statute is something that will be explained below. Given the nature of the Convention, it is unlikely that it would change at any point in the near future but it is always a good idea to consult the latest version. This can be accessed on the Council of Europe website, at www.echr.coe.int/Documents/Convention_ENG.pdf

You will note that this is not a domestic instrument, but rather an international treaty. In order for it to apply at the domestic level in the UK, this treaty needs to be 'incorporated'. The UK has a dualist system which has parliamentary sovereignty at its core. Being a 'dualist' system means that a country will need to, first, sign and commit to the treaty externally, but for it to have any domestic impact, there must, second, be a further incorporating instrument. As the UK has parliamentary sovereignty at the heart of its system, this instrument will need to be a statute. This statute is the Human Rights Act 1998. The consequence of this is that you will often be focused upon provisions of the Human Rights Act, rather than the Convention, despite the rights being contained in the Convention and not the Human Rights Act. This may seem like complex and irrelevant detail at this stage, but it is important to be precise in this area. You will need to understand the background of the Convention, but formulate an argument through the lens of the Human Rights Act. The only time this would change would be if you were mooting in an international setting. You can access legislation for free at www.legislation.gov.uk. This is a direct link to the Human Rights Act 1998: www.legislation.gov.uk/ukpga/1998/42/contents

A further area that requires precision is in considering which right(s) are at issue. There are two main ways in which rights may be questioned. An individual may argue that their rights have been breached, with the opposing side arguing that no breach took place. The typical Respondent in these cases is the state body and the argument will often be that they acted within their discretion. This is technically known as a state acting within their margin of appreciation. There may be a different argument, however, with individuals arguing that they have a right that outweighs another right. In such cases, the courts will need to 'balance' the conflicting rights. Although the Human Rights Act 1998 generally only applies to public bodies, in this second type of case, private parties can be involved. **Swifter and Handsworth v Daily Herald** shows how this can be the case.

In light of the above, we will now consider the argument that each advocate will make. Remember to remain focused on the particular ground of appeal and the precise angle that each advocate has been permitted to argue before the court.

The grounds of appeal in **Swifter and Handsworth v Daily Herald** are distinct again, as they are 'cumulative' arguments. Should the first ground fail, the second becomes irrelevant. This is because if the court finds on the first ground that the Appellants had no reasonable expectation of privacy (i.e. their rights under Article 8 were not engaged), there is no need to consider whether there is an overriding public interest in the information becoming public; if the first ground fails, then publication will be lawful. It is important to understand this when formulating your arguments and making sure the senior and junior arguments complement each other.

In **Swifter and Handsworth v Daily Herald**, the two grounds revolve around whether there has been a breach of the Appellants' right to respect for privacy regarding their wedding. Although both grounds are intrinsically linked, they have highly distinct angles of legal argument. The first ground focuses upon whether or not the Appellants had a reasonable expectation of privacy on their wedding day. The Respondent will, most obviously, be arguing that the Appellants' celebrity status etc. meant that they had no such expectation of privacy.

The second ground takes a different approach. In this ground, the Appellants are seeking to further protect their respect for privacy. There is a possibility, if such a right to respect for privacy is established, that it can be overridden, if so doing is in the public interest. The second ground seeks to deal with this possibility by arguing that no such overriding public interest exists; Swifter and Handsworth are arguing that their right to respect for privacy trumps the public's interest in seeing the photos and reading about the Appellants' behaviour at the wedding. The Respondent's argument on this will, no doubt, seek to focus on the importance of exposing the behaviour of Handsworth, in particular, in light of his clean-cut image and the perception of his character by the public.

Both of these grounds focus upon the right to respect for privacy. As such, they focus upon Article 8 of the European Convention on Human Rights, as incorporated by the Human Rights Act 1998:

ARTICLE 8

Right to respect for private and family life

1. *Everyone has the right to respect for his private and family life, his home and his correspondence.*

2. *There shall be no interference by a public authority with the exercise of this right except such as is in accordance with the law and is necessary in a democratic society in the interests of national security, public safety or the economic well-being of the country, for the prevention of disorder or crime, for the protection of health or morals, or for the protection of the rights and freedoms of others.*

The first ground will consider the parameters of the right to respect for privacy; whereas in the second ground of appeal, the court will need to balance the right to respect for privacy, against the 'right' of the Daily Herald to publish the photographs and stories. As such, this invokes Article 10 of the Convention, which protects freedom of expression. Essentially, the court must balance Article 10 against Article 8. Article 10 reads:

ARTICLE 10

Freedom of expression

1. *Everyone has the right to freedom of expression. This right shall include freedom to hold opinions and to receive and impart information and ideas without interference by public authority and regardless of frontiers. This Article shall not prevent States from requiring the licensing of broadcasting, television or cinema enterprises.*

2. *The exercise of these freedoms, since it carries with it duties and responsibilities, may be subject to such formalities, conditions, restrictions or penalties as are prescribed by law and are necessary in a democratic society, in the interests of national security, territorial integrity or public safety, for the prevention of disorder or crime, for the protection of health or morals, for the protection of the reputation or rights of others, for preventing the disclosure of information received in confidence, or for maintaining the authority and impartiality of the judiciary.*

The wording of Article 10(2), specifically 'necessary in a democratic society', will be of particular importance to the second ground. This is because the advocates will be arguing that publication of the photographs either is or is not necessary in a democratic society. The role of the press in furthering and supporting the existence of a democratic society is a popular concept within the European human rights framework.

This may seem complex as compared to the other moot problem questions, but the starting point for any moot will always be the same. Once again, ask yourself some simple questions to clarify your basic understanding of the ground of appeal given to you. For example, ask yourself:

- Am I arguing for the appeal to be allowed or dismissed?
- Am I arguing that Swifter and Handsworth had a reasonable expectation of privacy with regard to their wedding, or not?
- Am I arguing that there was an overriding public interest in publishing the information from Swifter and Handsworth's wedding?
- Or, am I arguing that the right to respect for privacy should trump the Daily Herald's right to publish the information?

Once you are comfortable with the answers to these questions, you should be in a position to identify search terms that can be used to start your legal research.

SELECTING YOUR RESEARCH TERMS

This section is designed to help you move from analysing the problem question into beginning your research. Again, Ali and Anna were directed to systematically select their research terms, including both obvious and hidden terms.

Senior Counsel

Below is Ali's attempt for the Senior Appellant:

Paragraph	Obvious Research Terms	Hidden Research Terms
1	private, image, secrecy, married	star, famous, well-known, private/privacy, secret
2	newspapers, photos, images, story, drug use, infidelity	newspaper, press, Facebook, Twitter, story/stories, publish, affair, drugs, illegal drugs, intoxicated, stoned

| 3 | right to privacy, infringement | human rights, ECHR, article 8, misuse of private information |
| 4 | reasonable expectation, public interest | freedom of press, freedom of expression, freedom of information |

In his selection of obvious terms, Ali has focused relatively narrowly on the first ground of appeal. This can be seen from his reference to privacy, what the Appellants allege should have been private (i.e. their wedding), and how they allege that privacy was violated (i.e. the publication of the wedding photos/stories by the Daily Herald). Notably, in paragraph four, Ali has identified the phrase 'reasonable expectation'. This is because he noted that this phrase sounded like legal terminology. This is the correct approach to take, especially with phrases linked to the grounds of appeal; however, Ali perhaps cut corners here by omitting to complete the phrase. This would have been better noted down as 'reasonable expectation *of privacy*'. This makes sense above anything else. This is because 'reasonable expectation' is not a phrase that makes sense in isolation. One must have a 'reasonable expectation' of something. All told, as underscored in all chapters, you should not 'chop up' the grounds of appeal.

In his hidden terms, Ali shows an awareness of synonyms. For example, for the term 'celebrity', he notes the terms 'star', 'famous' and 'well known'. However, he omits the term 'celebrity' itself, which is a gap in his research, as it is most likely that a court would use the term celebrity to cover all these labels. Ali also shows an awareness of different media outlets (for example, 'Twitter', 'Facebook', etc.), which may lead him to alternative case law. Most impressively, however, Ali uses his own legal knowledge to identify that this is a human rights related problem question and pinpoints the ECHR and Article 8, which is the most applicable right to the first ground of appeal.

Overall, Ali has made a useful attempt at identifying relevant terms, but he does make one glaring omission. Ali does not reference *Douglas v Hello! Ltd (No. 1)* [2001] 2 All ER 289 or *Campbell v Mirror Group Newspapers Ltd* [2004] UKHL 22, which were relied upon by the High Court in the instant case. The moot problem does not tell the advocates how the cases were relied upon, but this is irrelevant – the advocates must work it out. If case law is cited within a moot problem question, those references should always be a starting point for your research, whether that be by reading the cases first, or simply incorporating them into your initial, wider research. For example, by seeing how they are discussed (if at all) in an appropriate textbook. It is safe to say, any general human rights textbook would reference these two cases.

Anna prepared for the role of Senior Respondent. Below is her attempt:

Paragraph	Obvious Research Terms	Hidden Research Terms
1	young pop star, sexual provocative songs, dance routines, children's television presenter, clean cut image, married, private affair, secrecy, concern, disapproval	bad lifestyle, extreme behaviour, fear of criticism
2	ex-boyfriend, outraged, sell the story, newspaper, huge detail, lurid sex life, breakdown, increasing drug use, infidelity, printed story, pictures, details, wedding, intoxicated, using drugs, cocaine, smoking cannabis, teenage girls	previous partner, malicious act, hatred, unlawful drug use during the wedding, influencing youths, bad image, bad influence, in need of protection, famous on the news
3	infringement of the right to privacy	human rights breach, Article 8, right to respect private life and family
4	no reasonable expectations of privacy, manner, concerned courted the press, outweighed, drug use, young fans	not a breach of human rights, need to protect the public due to misbehaviour
5	Court of Appeal, upheld the judgment, appeal to the Supreme Court, reasonable expectation, privacy, wedding, relationship, photographs, public interest, drug use	court denied their arguments, all information is now published

In identifying her research terms, Anna has taken a fuller and broader approach than Ali in both categories. As a result, Anna will naturally need to take more time filtering her terms to ensure she undertakes efficient and useful research. Her selection of research terms, set out below, shows she did this well. The very fact Anna and Ali take such different approaches in relation to the same ground of appeal just goes to show how 'personal' a person's mooting can be. There is no right or wrong way of doing things. That said, Anna's most glaring omission is the same as Ali's: she did not read *Douglas* or *Campbell*. If she had done so, she could have identified more nuanced terms.

Junior Counsel

Taking into consideration Ali and Anna's different approaches, below is our attempt at selecting research terms for Junior Counsel. We have presented our terms from across the moot problem, not in relation to each paragraph. As always, our aim was to focus on the relevant ground of appeal and use our existing knowledge of the law to aid our efforts. Importantly, before we selected terms, we reviewed *Douglas* (www.bailii.org/ew/cases/EWCA/Civ/2000/353.html) and *Campbell* (www.bailii.org/uk/cases/UKHL/2004/22.html). This proved to be very helpful. We have put a * next to the terms we identified through our reading of these cases. Notably, it soon became clear that *Douglas* related more closely to ground one of the appeal and *Campbell* related more closely to ground two of the appeal.

Obvious Research Terms	Hidden Research Terms
famous, wedding, clean-cut image, drugs, sex life, secrecy, photographs, printed, public interest, public interest in publication, Campbell, Mirror Group Newspapers, newspaper	freedom of expression, private information*, confidential information*, breach of confidence*, misled the public*, margin of appreciation*, Article 10, set the record straight*, Human Rights Act 1998

Campbell similarly led us to the concept of confidential information and breach of confidence. It also confirmed that our legal terminology – Article 10, freedom of expression and margin of appreciation – was correctly included. More importantly, the case led us to phrases that linked with the Daily Herald's argument that the publication of the relevant material was in the public interest. This was because the published material would arguably 'set the record straight' because Handsworth's 'clean cut' image was misleading to the public in light of what was shown by the photos depicting his drug use. The summary of the *Campbell* case provided below will make this point clearer.

SUMMARY

In this section we have shown you how to analyse a human rights law moot problem question. We have done this by, first, deconstructing the problem question to highlight its fundamental features. We have then demonstrated approaches to summarising the problem question, interpreting the grounds of appeal and generating initial research terms. We will utilise these research terms in the next section, which focuses on how to carry out appropriate legal research for **Swifter and Handsworth v Daily Herald**.

RESEARCH

This section focuses on how to research the areas of law related to **Swifter and Handsworth v Daily Herald**. This problem question differs from the previous two as it includes the Human Rights Act 1998 and requires the advocates to engage with non-domestic case law and an international instrument, namely the European Convention of Human Rights. The case continues to focus, however, on judicial interpretation of certain legal principles, the key one being privacy. This section will focus, therefore, on identifying, interpreting and applying cases that are relevant in this area, as well as understanding the relevance of the Human Rights Act and how it should be used before the court.

Before going on to consider the specific research Ali and Anna undertook for this case, you should remind yourself of the preliminary considerations for researchers that we set out on page 14.

RESEARCHING SWIFTER AND HANDSWORTH V DAILY HERALD

The rules in relation to **Swifter and Handsworth v Daily Herald** allowed Ali and Anna each to use three cases (including any non-domestic cases), any relevant legislation and two 'other' sources, such as scholarship.

Both students' research trails actually show what a simple problem this is to research, if you properly analyse the problem question and select appropriate search terms first. This moot was about four things:

- a celebrity wedding
- the couple's expectations of privacy for that wedding
- unauthorised publication of photographs of a controversial nature by a newspaper
- the newspaper's belief that publication was in the public interest.

The problem question tells us all of this. The relevant information can be garnered from the first two paragraphs dealing with the facts, with the specialised terminology surfacing in the grounds of appeal. This shows you that if you carefully read and analyse a problem, often everything you need is right there.

In varying ways, Ali and Anna both fastened onto this. Their research trails for ground one of the appeal show this through very specific use of terms and a smooth ride through to relevant sources.

Below is a list of Ali and Anna's most common research terms:

Ali	Anna
• human rights	• infringement of privacy
• privacy	• human rights
• newspaper	• famous
• press	• celebrity
• wedding	• privacy
• injunction	• wedding
• public interest	• story
• private and family life	• public
• image	
• publish	

You will see that all of these terms relate very closely to the four crucial components of the question we outline above. These research terms generated the following sources, which are patently applicable to the grounds of appeal, as will be seen in the summaries below.

Ali	Anna
• European Convention of Human Rights, Article 8	• *Trimingham v Associated Newspapers Ltd* [2012] EWHC 1296 QB
• *Douglas v Hello! Ltd (No. 1)* [2001] 2 All ER 289	• *Campbell v Mirror Group Newspapers Ltd* [2004] UKHL 22
• *Campbell v Mirror Group Newspapers Ltd* [2004] UKHL 22	• *Douglas v Hello! Ltd (No. 1)* [2001] 2 All ER 289
• *Von Hannover v Germany*, Appl No 40660/08 and 60641/08 [2012] 55 EHRR 15	• *Murray v Express Newspapers Plc* [2008] EWCA Civ 446
• *Murray v Express Newspapers PLC* [2008] EWCA Civ 446	• Human Rights Act 1998.
	• European Convention of Human Rights, Article 8(1) and (2)

Evidently, Ali and Anna planned to use some of the same sources. This makes total sense given they are researching the same ground of appeal. You will see from our efforts in relation to ground two of the appeal, however, the same legal instruments and cases appear again. This goes to show the overlapping nature of the grounds of appeal or, as we explained earlier, the interdependence of them. All of the advocates will be using the Human Rights Act 1998 and the Convention. The advocates will be using largely the same case law, but for different purposes. On the one hand, ground one is concerned with how the cases address what circumstances do and do not lead to the existence of a 'reasonable expectation of privacy' in particular circumstances (such as a wedding). On the other hand, ground two is concerned with how the cases address how and when this expectation can be 'trumped' by the existence of circumstances that mean invading this privacy is in the public interest.

SUMMARISING YOUR RESEARCH

Summarising the products of your research is a useful way to begin thinking about the contours of your arguments.

We have already set out the text of Articles 8 and 10 for you on page 94.

Below are extracts from sections of the Human Rights Act 1998, which will be particularly useful for the advocates in **Swifter and Handsworth v Daily Herald**. You should think about how they would allow the advocates to contextualise the appeal for the court.

Human Rights Act 1998 Section 1(1)(a)

(1) In this Act 'the Convention rights' means the rights and fundamental freedoms set out in—

Articles 2 to 12 and 14 of the Convention.

Human Rights Act 1998 Section 2(1)

Interpretation of Convention rights.

(1) A court or tribunal determining a question which has arisen in connection with a Convention right must take into account any—

(a) judgment, decision, declaration or advisory opinion of the European Court of Human Rights,

(b) opinion of the Commission given in a report adopted under Article 31 of the Convention,

(c) decision of the Commission in connection with Articles 26 or 27(2) of the Convention, or

(d) decision of the Committee of Ministers taken under Article 46 of the Convention,

whenever made or given, so far as, in the opinion of the court or tribunal, it is relevant to the proceedings in which that question has arisen.

Source	Summary	Ground One Relevance	Ground Two Relevance
Douglas v Hello! Ltd (No. 1) (2001) 2 All ER 289	Michael Douglas and Catherine Zeta Jones (two famous actors) got married and signed a contract with OK! Magazine for the exclusive rights to wedding images. Hello! Magazine ascertained their own images and wished to publish them. An injunction, preventing publication, was imposed on Hello! Magazine. This case addressed the balance of rights between Douglas and Hello! Magazine. The Court of Appeal found in favour of Hello! Magazine and lifted the injunction.	This case does not (other than once) reference the phrase 'reasonable expectation of privacy'. This does not mean it is irrelevant to this ground, however. This case deals with the idea that a personal right to privacy exists in English law, in the sense that a person can protect against unwanted intrusion in certain, private aspects of their life. For the purposes of ground one, how the court assesses the nature of the private sphere attached to the Douglas wedding, in light of other facts, provides assistance to the advocates dealing with this ground.	This case has a more explicit connection with ground two, in that it makes more direct references to 'freedom of expression' and 'public interest'. This case therefore provides direction on how the court will undertake the balancing act when confronted with competing rights concerning privacy and freedom of expression.

| *Campbell v Mirror Group Newspapers Ltd* [2004] UKHL 22 | Naomi Campbell, a famous model, was challenging the publication of a story about her attendance at Narcotics Anonymous meetings, together with covertly taken images. Campbell had previously denied stories of drug taking and claimed that such publication breached her right to privacy. The House of Lords allowed Campbell's appeal. The House of Lords found that the Court of Appeal had been incorrect to find that *all* published information fell within the margin of appreciation left to journalists. In other words, the journalists had crossed the line in relation to some of the published material. The court, therefore, determined that Campbell's right to privacy outweighed the Mirror Group's right to freedom of expression in relation to certain material. | The House of Lords questioned the extent to which someone would have a 'reasonable expectation of privacy' in particular with regard to photographs that had been taken. This consideration was had both generally and with regard to photographs taken in a public place. The court considered, in particular, the different attributes of the claimant. The key statement was made by Lord Hope, who stated that: 'The question is what a reasonable person of ordinary sensibilities would feel if she was placed in the same position as the claimant and faced the same publicity.'

In this case, and many that follow, the cases turn on their own facts. The court must consider the attributes of the claimant, along with the complete circumstances of the alleged breach. | The court found that there would not be a public interest in publication of images and information simply by virtue of Campbell's fame. While the court agreed that Campbell's previous discussion of drug use and the correction of her statements would have had some public interest, it disagreed that the amount of information and the images were all necessary to achieve this. In the instant case, advocates therefore would need to be aware of the celebrity status of the Appellants as well as the image they portray to the public. This information would be relevant to reasoning on this ground. |

continued

Source	Summary	Ground One Relevance	Ground Two Relevance
		The Appellants in **Swifter and Handsworth v Daily Herald** could use the majority judgment. This was, however a 3–2 majority decision so the Respondents could utilise the reasoning of Lord Hoffman and Lord Nicholls.	
Murray v Express Newspapers Plc [2008] EWCA Civ 446	Murray was the infant son of a famous author. His photograph was taken in a public place and subsequently published. Murray challenged this publication, through his parents. Murray's appeal was allowed. The fact that the photographs were taken in public did not, automatically, rule out a claim to privacy.	The case turned on the extent to which Murray had a reasonable expectation of privacy that would mean publication of images taken in public would breach this right. The court considered that to make a determination on whether there was a reasonable expectation of privacy, all circumstances of the case must be considered. This included 'the attributes of the claimant, the nature of the activity in which the claimant was engaged, the place at which it was happening, the nature and purpose of the intrusion, the	The court showed recognition that there would be an 'interest' in seeing images of the claimant, as the son of a famous author. They also reasoned, however, that the simple fact of his mother being famous did not necessarily mean that there was a public interest in publication of images and information about him. Advocates need to appreciate that fame will not, in itself, mean that all facets of someone's life can be narrated in the press. There must be a public interest in *the particular material* published.

		absence of consent and whether it was known or could be inferred, the effect on the claimant and the circumstances in which and the purposes for which the information came into the hands of the publisher'. Advocates for both Appellant and Respondent must take these factors into consideration when approaching the question of reasonable expectation of privacy.	For example, in the instant case, there should not be an argument on public interest made purely on the basis that the Appellant is a celebrity. The argument needs to be more nuanced than that, with considerations of the specific nature of the information conveyed, i.e. the portrayal of drug use.
Trimingham v Associated Newspapers Ltd [2012] EWHC 1296 QB	Trimingham claimed damages and an injunction against a newspaper publisher for infringement of her privacy rights. The claimant had an affair with a married Member of Parliament, while she was in a civil partnership.	The claimant complained that her 'reasonable expectation of privacy' had been breached by the publication of numerous articles.	The court engages in common law surrounding 'freedom of expression' providing a selection of cases the advocates could use to shape their own arguments on this point.

continued

105

Source	Summary	Ground One Relevance	Ground Two Relevance
	Numerous articles appeared in newspapers and in an online paper making references to the claimant's sexuality and appearance. Photographs taken on the day of the claimant's civil partnership were published in newspapers. The appeal was dismissed.	The court engages with the concept that, while there is often a reasonable expectation of privacy in relation to details about a sexual or family relationship, 'the position is not the same in respect of the bare fact of a sexual relationship'. In so doing, the court engages with the *Murray and Campbell* decisions, concerning what factors are relevant when assessing the existence of a 'reasonable expectation of privacy'. The court held, in this case, the claimant did not have a 'reasonable expectation of privacy' in relation to her sexuality and the ending of her civil partnership because it was mere fact that was already in the public domain.	The court found it 'would be a serious interference with freedom of expression if those wishing to express their own views could be silenced by, or threatened with, claims for harassment based on subjective claims by individuals that they felt offended or insulted'. The court found that the nature of the complaints made by the claimant did not make it necessary or proportionate to prohibit publication.

| *Von Hannover v Germany*, Appl No 40660/08 and 60641/08 [2012] 55 EHRR 15. | Princess Caroline of Monaco and her husband appealed to the European Court of Human Rights against the refusal of the German courts to grant an injunction against publication of photographs taken of the couple walking down a street whilst on a skiing holiday. The photographs were taken when Prince Rainier, her father and the reigning monarch, was ill at home. The Royal couple argued that further publication of the images would not contribute to a debate of public interest. The ECtHR dismissed the appeal, finding *inter alia* that the German courts properly balanced the right of the publishing companies to freedom of expression against the Royal couple's right to respect for their private life. The appeal was dismissed. | The ECtHR engaged in the concept of 'privacy' under Article 8. The court underscored that the concept extends to aspects relating to a personal identity, including photographs taken of them, and their moral integrity.

The court's engagement with these ideas could guide an advocate about how the images in the instant case might have attached to them a 'reasonable expectation of privacy'. | The ECtHR reviews factors relevant to the balancing act to be carried out between competing Article 8 and 10 rights, in the context of the unauthorised publication of photographs of a famous couple. The judgment therefore provides advocates dealing with this ground of appeal guidance on what considerations are relevant when undertaking this assessment. The advocate can then apply these factors to the instant case, as appropriate from their client's perspective. |

The above summaries are designed to show you how the case law identified by Ali and Anna can inform both grounds of appeal. They also highlight how straightforward researching the problem was here. Both students selected useful search terms, filtering their more extensive lists skilfully, and generated useful sources of law as a consequence.

The above summaries show the key ways in which advocates can use these important cases. They also highlight some important factors to be aware of, however:

- **The cases above are extremely fact-sensitive**. Each case turns on its specific facts, and the advocates must pay attention to this. Advocates must also pay close attention to the narrow findings of the courts, in that a court may find publication of some material appropriate and some not. *Campbell* demonstrates this.
- **These cases also remind advocates to not be solely guided by 'hard' outcomes, i.e. the actual outcome of the claim, but rather the reasoning behind it**. *Campbell* is a great example of this, with the House of Lords' decision being a majority one of 3–2.
- **The jurisprudence of the ECtHR jurisprudence can be instructive to domestic cases**. The *Von Hannover* case provides an example of this. Advocates must remind themselves of how to explain and use such case law within English courts.
- **Conducting wider research for context purposes is sometimes necessary**. For example, public interest dimensions in *Von Hannover* make better sense once the advocate has an idea about the relationship shared by the Von Hannovers and Prince Ranier III. Similarly, the public interest arguments in the *Trimingham* case become clearer once you understand the professional relationship between an MP and an aide.

SUMMARY

This section has shown how straightforward research can be when a mooter selects appropriate terms to undertake their research with. It also shows how important it is to carefully analyse your selected sources and appreciate how they inform each ground of appeal.

ARGUMENT CONSTRUCTION

Ali and Anna selected very helpful authorities after carefully selecting research terms. However, this exercise is meaningless if the authorities are not then carefully analysed and appropriately applied to the relevant grounds of appeal. By not taking such a careful approach in cases where attention to detail is crucial, any argument constructed by an advocate will have substantial weaknesses. This is evident when we look respectively at Ali and Anna's arguments for the Senior Appellant and Senior Respondent. In short, great authorities do not automatically lead to a great argument. The advocate must shape them accordingly.

The mistakes made by Ali and Anna, however, provide us with a great opportunity to underscore the importance of understanding your authorities and ground of appeal. At this point you should remind yourself of the 'Preliminary Considerations for Constructing a Skeleton Argument' as set out on page 29. This section will provide feedback on the draft submissions Ali and Anna constructed for the first ground of appeal, and then provide sample skeleton submissions for the second ground of appeal, along with a rationale for our approach. Please note, that we include additional authorities in our submissions. You should ensure that you review and understand these cases and their relevance.

SUBMISSIONS FOR THE APPELLANT

We will first of all consider how Ali developed submissions for the Senior Appellant.

Ali, as Senior Appellant, would be arguing:

> *Milly Swifter and Laurence Handsworth's rights under Article 8 ECHR were engaged and, therefore, they* did *have a reasonable expectation of privacy and, consequently, their right to privacy* had *been breached.*

Below shows what Ali's skeleton for the Senior Appellant would have looked like using his first draft submissions. You should consider the feedback we provide about his submissions and think about what it shows about the weaknesses in his argument construction. We then provide sample submissions for the Junior Appellant, with an accompanying rationale for our approach.

IN THE SUPREME COURT OF THE UNITED KINGDOM

Swifter and Handsworth v Daily Herald

Appellants' Skeleton Argument

Senior Counsel for the Appellant shall submit:

Ground One:

1. The Appellants did have a reasonable expectation of privacy during their wedding. Their claims should be upheld because of the nature of the activities in which they were engaged, the likely effect the publication would have on them and the absence of their consent. See: *Murray v Express Newspapers Plc* **[2008] EWCA Civ 446** and *Von Hannover v Germany,* **Appl No 40660/08 and 60641/08 [2012] 55 EHRR 15.**

Feedback: This submission is phrased in too general terms. Ali needs to be more specific about the Appellants' 'claims', 'conduct' and the 'effect' publication would have on them. Ali has not linked the concept of 'reasonable expectation of privacy' to the authorities he references, and is not clear on how he wishes the court to use those authorities. For instance, Ali should be underscoring that Murray sets out a test for determining when a 'reasonable expectation of privacy' exists.

2. The importance of the Appellants' right to privacy is not outweighed by any other external factor, such as the potential criminal enquiries their activities may lead to or the irresponsible nature of their behaviour in front of young fans. *Campbell v Mirror Group Newspapers Ltd* **[2004] UKHL 22**. Furthermore, the Appellants' wish for complete secrecy demonstrates that the judge's reasoning for dismissing their claim was faulty at first instance. *Douglas v Hello! Ltd (No. 1)* **[2001] 2 All ER 289.**

Feedback: This submission actually makes two separate arguments. The first relates to how Ali wants the court to apply the case of Campbell. However, Ali does not make his position clear. Ali needs to connect judicial comments about exposing criminal activity in Campbell to his argument about the existence of a 'reasonable expectation of privacy'. The way Ali has phrased this part of his submission, and, in particular, his use of the word 'outweighed', gives the impression he may stray into ground two of the appeal. This is a clear example of what can happen if advocates do not choose their words carefully. What Ali actually means to argue is that the potential criminal activity of the Appellants does not negate their reasonable expectation of privacy. Ali's second argument relates to how he wishes the court to consider the case of Douglas, but again he is not clear. His phrasing is awkward. What

Ali actually means to argue is that the very secret nature of the Appellants'
wedding distinguishes it from Douglas, and Douglas should, therefore, not be
applied in the instant case.

3. The court should allow this appeal on the basis that, as the Appellants are
    well-known to the public, the publications are likely to cause harm to their
    reputation and possibly to their careers. It would therefore be unreasona-
    ble to dismiss the appeal on the basis of Art 10 (*Campbell v Mirror
    Group Newspapers Ltd*), and it would be ultra vires to do so as *Von
    Hannover v Germany* is a binding authority.

Feedback: This submission is, again, poorly phrased. There does not seem to be
much basis or foundation to Ali's initial point and it is not clear how his initial argu-
ment would lead to it being 'unreasonable' to dismiss the appeal. The inclusion of
a throwaway sentence on a European Court of Human Rights case (Von Hannover)
is also poor as it does not fully engage with the relationship between this court and
the domestic court. Moreover, Ali's reference to Article 10 suggests his argument
could stray into ground two of the appeal. Ali has, again, omitted any direction on
how his authorities should be used by the court.

Now consider our submissions for the Junior Appellant below. The crux of
this ground of appeal, for the Junior Appellant, is that any public interest in
publishing the photographs, which is protected under Article 10, is outweighed by the Appellants' right to respect for privacy under Article 8.

Junior Counsel for the Appellant shall submit:

Ground Two:
1. The Appellant has made no *'untrue pronouncements'* concerning his life-
    style and therefore the publication of the photos and related information is
    not in the public interest. This Court should distinguish from the decision
    of the Court of Appeal in *Campbell v Mirror Group Newspapers Ltd*
    [2004] UKHL 22.

Rationale: We address the case of Campbell in our first submission because it was
an authority used by the lower court in the instant case. As such, it is clearly
important to the instant appeal. We are clear how we wish the instant court to con-
sider Campbell and on what basis. In effect, we are arguing because in the case of
Campbell the Appellant did make 'untrue pronouncements' about herself (i.e. that
she had never used drugs), and in this case the Appellants did not (at least not in
categorical terms), the case should not be followed.

2. Neither **Article 8** nor **Article 10** (as incorporated by the **Human Rights Act 1998**) has precedence over the other, therefore this court must undertake a 'balancing exercise'. In ***Von Hannover v Germany*, Appl No 40660/08 and 60641/08 [2012] 55 EHRR 15** the Grand Chamber established that the decisive factor in the balance between these Articles is 'the contribution which the publication makes to a debate of general interest'. The Appellants' private life is of no general interest and therefore this Court should not weigh this balance in favour of **Article 10**.

Rationale: We are clear about how Articles 8 and 10 are positioned in English law, and about what the court must do in the event that the rights in those articles conflict. We then use Von Hannover to underscore what factor is most crucial to the balancing exercise that the court must undertake. Note that we highlight that the case was decided by the Grand Chamber, the highest chamber of the European Court of Human Rights, in order to underscore how important the decision is. We then clearly apply that factor to the instant case, in favour of the Appellant.

3. The publication of the story and photographs exceeds '*the essential function of the press in a democratic society*'. See ***Krone Verlag GmbH & Co KG v Austria* [2003] 36 EHRR 57**. The information published by the Respondent is merely 'intended to titillate and entertain' and to 'satisfy the curiosity of a particular readership'. As per ***Mosley v UK* [2012] EMLR 1** '*such reporting does not attract the robust protection of Article 10*'.

Rationale: Using direct quotes from the cited cases we underscore our point that the publication of the photographs was not in the public interest. This is, first, because publication went beyond the essential function of the press, as per Krone. Second, as per Mosely, because the story was mere entertainment that was meant to embarrass the Appellants. We clearly connect our authorities to the ground of appeal and our argument, leaving the judge with no immediate uncertainty about the nature of our argument.

SUBMISSIONS FOR THE RESPONDENT

We will now consider Anna's submissions for the Respondent. As Senior Respondent, Anna will be arguing:

Milly Swifter and Laurence Handsworth's rights under Article 8 ECHR were not engaged and, therefore, they did not have a reasonable expectation of privacy and, consequently, their right to privacy had not been breached.

Below shows what Anna's skeleton would have looked like using her first draft submissions. Again, you should consider the feedback we provide and how it highlights the weaknesses in Anna's approach. We also provide sample submissions for the Junior Respondent, with an accompanying rationale for our approach.

IN THE SUPREME COURT OF THE UNITED KINGDOM

Swifter and Handsworth v Daily Herald

Respondent's Skeleton Argument

Senior Counsel for the Respondent shall submit:

Ground One:

1. The Appellants' right of privacy was not breached and they should not expect privacy in regards to their relationship, wedding and pictures taken as they are targeted by the media and Milly's actions draw attention. Thus, as in the case of ***Trimingham v Associated Newspapers Ltd* [2012] EWHC 1296 QB**, there is no infringement of their rights. ***Douglas v Hello! Ltd (No. 1)* [2001] 2 All ER 289.**

Feedback: To improve this submission, Anna needs to link the principle of a 'reasonable expectation of privacy' to the authorities that she cites. At the moment, it is not clear what principle she is using or how she is seeking to use the case law. You would, for example, expect Anna to be arguing that the court should follow Douglas, but she does not say this. She could also improve upon her phrasing as the submission is generally vague.

2. The couple's actions (use of illegal substances) were illegal and inappropriate. Laurence has misled the public into believing that he has a 'clean cut image', even though the publication of the wedding photographs indicated that, in fact, he has not. Thus, there is no violation of their rights in regards to the photographs as in the case of ***Campbell v Mirror Group Newspapers Ltd* [2004] UKHL 22**.

Feedback: Anna has strayed into a principle that is part of ground two, or is at least giving the impression of this through her written submission. She appears to be discussing the correction of the portrayal of an inaccurate public image, which is part of ground two; it is in the public interest to correct a false image. The case of Campbell makes this point. A more appropriate way for Anna to use the illegal activity of the Appellants to her advantage would be to argue that Article 8 should not afford 'a reasonable expectation of privacy' when an individual is engaged in criminal conduct. Campbell could be used to make this point.

3. The need to protect the wider public in accordance with **Art. 8(2) of the Human Rights Act 1998** outweighs the couple's right of privacy in regards to the photographs taken, their wedding and relationship.

Feedback: Anna makes a fundamental error here. Her written submission suggests a lack of understanding of the basics. Anna mentions 'Article 8(2) of the Human Rights Act 1998'. This is incorrect. She should be dealing with Article 8(2) of the European Convention as incorporated into English law by the Human Rights Act 1998. This may seem picky but an error like this gives the impression that the advocate has a fundamental lack of understanding. Regardless of this error, the submission overall is weak as it is unclear exactly what Anna intends to argue.

In addition to the above, Anna has seemingly omitted to tell the court that a legal test exists for determining when a 'reasonable expectation of privacy' exists. This test is set out in **Murray v Express Newspapers plc and another** *[2008]* **EWCA Civ 446***. Despite locating this case, Anna has omitted to use it.*

Now consider our submissions for the Junior Respondent below. The crux of this ground of appeal, for the Respondent, is that the public interest in seeing the photographs outweighs any right of the Appellant to respect for privacy under Article 8.

Junior Counsel for the Respondent shall submit:

Ground Two:

1. The right to respect for private and family life, contained in **Article 8 of the European Convention on Human Rights**, is a qualified right. This right can be outweighed by the right to freedom of expression, contained in **Article 10**, where the publication of material would be in the public interest. In a democratic society, the right to freedom of expression is especially important. The case of ***Von Hannover v Germany*, Appl No 40660/08 and 60641/08 [2012] 55 EHRR 15** should be followed.

Rationale: The purpose of this submission is to emphasise to the court the importance of Article 10 in a democratic society. This is simply a tactic. The idea is to put it in the court's mind from the very start that special importance should be attached to freedom of expression. Again, we back up our point by using a relevant case and make it clear what we want the court to do with that case.

2. When a 'celebrity' portrays a false image of their character, it is in the public interest to correct that false image. The Respondent urges this court to follow *Ferdinand v MGN Ltd* **[2011] EWHC 2454 (QB)** and *Campbell v Mirror Group Newspapers Ltd* **[2004] UKHL 22**. The Appellant (Handsworth) portrays a false image of himself, and therefore it is in the public interest to correct that image, especially given the Appellant's position as a role model for young people, and his conduct at the wedding was criminal.

Rationale: This is a classic example of a submission that showcases three fundamental lawyering skills, namely an ability to explain the law, cite relevant legal authority and apply both things to the instant case facts. We start by concisely laying out the legal principle concerning the correction of a false image, support that principle with relevant authorities and then directly apply both to the instant case. We use Ferdinand and Campbell for the end result (i.e. the court in those cases found Article 10 should be favoured) but also because they provide favourable factual comparisons. Both cases involve defendants who are role models for young people, and Campbell also involves criminal conduct being exposed. On this basis, we can shape a logical argument that this court should follow them.

3. As per Baroness Hale in *Campbell*, '*the possession and use of illegal drugs is a criminal offence and a matter of serious public concern. The press must be free to expose the truth and put the record straight.*' Given the influence the Appellants can have on younger audiences, it is even more important that the Respondent be able to set the record straight and expose their true character.

Rationale: We quote the words of Baroness Hale to underscore the argument that where criminal conduct is concerned, there is even more need for the press to expose the 'truth' and correct a false image. As such, our third submission follows on directly from our second. We then apply this statement directly to the instant case, integrating Baroness Hale's words where possible.

You should compare Ali and Anna's draft submissions to our submissions. In particular, you should pay close attention to the careful construction of our sentences and clarity of argument. Our submissions should not leave you confused about what we will argue and upon what authority. In addition, you should note how we engage different tactics to bolster our arguments, for example, by underscoring what court a case was decided by and by quoting directly from judgments. Finally, appreciate how our submissions are cosmetically consistent, making our submissions attractive in form as well as in substance.

THINKING AHEAD AND BEING CRITICAL

Once your submissions are drafted, you must start to think critically about your argument. This involves thinking ahead to what sorts of questions the judge might ask you during the course of your moot. The two concepts are closely related because the judge will seek to clarify and test your arguments.

General questions about each ground of appeal

This section considers some general questions a judge could ask the advocates about this appeal. These questions are designed to get you thinking about some of the broader legal concepts related to this appeal, and how to explain them with precision and clarity, and, where possible, relate the answer to the instant case. For each question, we provide some guidance on giving an appropriate answer.

- *What is the relationship between the European Convention of Human Rights and the Human Rights Act 1998?*

Guidance: This question is designed to test whether an advocate understands the distinction and relationship between these two legal instruments. A good answer would be something like this:

The European Convention of Human Rights is an international treaty to which the UK is a party. The Human Rights Act was passed in 1998 in order to incorporate the ECHR into domestic law. This means that rights in the ECHR are only enforceable in UK courts via the Human Rights Act.

- *What does it mean when a person says that Articles 8 and 10 of the European Convention of Human Rights have been 'incorporated' into English law?*

Guidance: This question is designed to see whether an advocate understands the term 'incorporation' in this specific context. A good answer would build on the knowledge in the above question and would be something like this:

Incorporation of any rights within the ECHR has been done via the Human Rights Act. This means that they can have legal effect within UK courts. Prior to the Human Rights Act, the UK was still bound by these rights but without incorporation such rights could only be enforced externally at the European Court of Human Rights.

- *What is the difference between a qualified and absolute right in the context of the European Convention of Human Rights?*

Guidance: This question is designed to check whether an advocate appreciates the different types of rights within the convention. A good answer would be something like this:

> Most rights within the ECHR are qualified rights. This means that they can be lawfully derogated from in certain circumstances. Articles 8 and 10 would be examples of qualified rights. Absolute rights can never be derogated from. The clearest example of this is freedom from torture.

- *What does the concept of the 'margin of appreciation' refer to?*

Guidance: This question is designed to check whether an advocate appreciates the discretion that a state has in implementation of rights. A good answer would be something like:

> The margin of appreciation allows a degree of discretion on the part of a state in its implementation of rights. It recognises that there are differing cultural and social contexts within the member states of the Council of Europe and does not require each interpretation of each right to be identical. Clearly in the instant appeal, the focus will be on the UK's interpretation of Articles 8 and 10 in this context.

- *When undertaking a balancing exercise between Articles 8 and 10, what factors can a court consider?*

Guidance: This question is designed to check whether an advocate understands the detail of the case law surrounding Articles 8 and 10. A good answer would direct the court to a specific case that has been cited within their skeleton that gives examples of factors to consider.

- *Are decisions of the European Court of Human Rights binding on this court?*

Guidance: This question is designed to check whether an advocate understands the relationship between the European Court of Human Rights and domestic courts. A good answer would explain that there is no specifically binding nature of judgments, but rather that s2 Human Rights Act requires courts to 'take into account' judgments of the European Court.

Specific questions about case law

As this moot is so fact-sensitive, it is worth considering what specific questions a judge could ask an advocate about the case law cited in this case. These questions are designed to make you consider a variety of themes, ranging from how to explain sensitive facts and specific legal concepts, to how to relate specific facts of cases to the instant case, and deal with more general questions about wider issues.

Douglas v Hello! Ltd (No. 1) [2001] 2 All ER 289

- *Douglas contracted with OK! Magazine to publish photographs from his wedding. What, if anything, does that tell us about how private they wished their wedding to be? And how is that different/similar to the instant case?*
- *The Douglas case centres on a claim of breach of confidence. In a legal sense, what is a 'breach of confidence'?*

Campbell v Mirror Group Newspapers Ltd [2004] UKHL 22

- *Was the court unanimous in its decision in this case? If not, how was the court split in terms of numbers and the nature of the judicial opinions?*
- *The court agreed publication was lawful in relation to some of the material in this case. What was the court's view about when the press 'crossed the line' into unlawful publication in this case?*
- *Does a celebrity not choose to compromise their own Article 8 rights?*

Von Hannover v Germany, Appl No 40660/08 and 60641/08 [2012] 55 EHRR 15

- *This case concerned members of a royal family. The public interest in publishing the relevant material in this case related, in part, to the fact that they were historical figures. How does that view relate to this case?*
- *Did the Grand Chamber make any comments about the fact that the photos had already been published in this case?*

Murray v Express Newspapers PLC [2008] EWCA Civ 446

- *Is the 'reasonable expectation of privacy' test in Murray objective or subjective?*
- *How does the test apply to the instant case?*
- *Does the fact that the Murray case concerned publication of images of a child make it distinguishable from the instant case?*

Trimingham v Associated Newspapers Ltd (2012) EWHC 1296 QB

- *What did the relevant photographs in Trimingham depict exactly?*
- *Do you think that the comments made about Trimingham, by the press, were unkind?*
- *Should the 'kindness' of press headlines play any role in this court's decision-making?*

Krone Verlag GmbH & Co KG v Austria [2003] 36 EHRR 57

- *This case concerned restrictions placed on advertising. How does it relate to the instant case?*
- *Did the European Court of Human Rights find there was a violation of Article 10 in this case?*

Mosley v UK [2012] EMLR 1

- *How would you describe the pictures published in Moseley?*
- *The court said the pictures in Moseley were merely intended to entertain and embarrass the subject of them. How does that relate to the instant case?*

Ferdinand v MGN Ltd [2011] EWHC 2454 (QB)

- *Do the Appellants in the instant cases share any similarities with Mr Ferdinand?*
- *Do you think every facet of the life of a 'celebrity' is open to public scrutiny?*

SUMMARY

Constructing a clear and logical argument that addresses the grounds of appeal in a comprehensive way, which accounts for both their strengths and weaknesses, is vital to preparing to moot successfully.

It is also important to remember that the construction of your skeleton argument and your critical assessment of it is just one step (albeit a significant one) in preparing to advocate. Once you have completed this process, it is time to develop your extended oral presentation. We provide some guidance on how to do this in the final chapter of the book.

When constructing your argument in a human rights case, you need to be sure that you understand the different legal instruments at play. If there is any lack of understanding in the legal instruments and their interrelationship, then this will become glaringly obvious and you will end up with large holes in your work. You should also be sure to understand the fact-specific nature of the relevant cases here. The courts will always be reluctant to make any broad, sweeping judgments and any argument should take account of this fact-specific approach.

CONCLUSION

In this chapter, we have shown you how to analyse, research and construct an argument in relation to the moot problem presented by the fictitious case of **Swifter and Handsworth v Daily Herald**.

4 CONTRACT LAW

INTRODUCTION

In this chapter, we will show you how to analyse, research and construct an argument in relation to the moot problem presented by the fictitious case of **Aston v Finn**. This is a contract law themed moot problem question.

This first section will focus on analysing the moot problem. It will begin by deconstructing the problem question and introduce you to its basic, but fundamental, features. Next, it will focus on summarising the problem question. It will then consider how to interpret the grounds of appeal and the angle you should take for your allocated role. Finally, it will examine how to derive search terms from a problem question, to allow you to progress on to researching the relevant area of law.

In this question, Ali undertook the roles of Senior Appellant and Senior Respondent, and Anna prepared for the roles of Junior Appellant and Junior Respondent.

ANALYSIS

THE PROBLEM QUESTION

A **IN THE SUPREME COURT OF THE UNITED KINGDOM**

ASTON **B**

V

FINN **C**

Alfred Finn is the owner of a block of ten luxury penthouse apartments. He bought the entire complex – which he named Tulip Place – from a property developer called Cosy Homes Ltd in March 2012. He bought the complex empty and quickly arranged for the apartments to be filled with tenants. Each **D** apartment had a rent of £1,200/month. In April 2012 he entered into a contract with Les Aston, a local painter, under which Mr Aston agreed to paint the ten apartments in 15 days in return for a fee of £10,000. Mr Aston commenced work on time on Monday 7 May 2012 as required by the contract.

On the afternoon of Friday 11 May, as Mr Aston was leaving the site, he told Mr Finn that he would see him on Monday morning. Mr Finn asked why he was not coming in to work on Saturday. Mr Aston responded that he was not required by the terms of the contract to work at weekends. Mr Finn pointed out that he had new tenants moving into all of the apartments on Wednesday 23 May. This made it vital that the work be completed by 6pm on Tuesday 22 May. He also insisted that the terms of the contract expressly required Mr Aston to work at weekends. Mr Aston denied this, but neither party could find a copy of the contract to resolve the dispute.

A heated argument broke out between the two men. Mr Aston demanded an extra £3,000 before he would even consider working at the weekend, telling Mr Finn that he would have his men 'down paint brushes right now!' Mr Finn refused to pay, insisting that he would not be blackmailed. Eventually Mr Finn agreed to pay Mr Aston an extra £1,500 to work over the weekend and to complete the work by 6pm on Tuesday 22 May. He did this one hour after both men left the site on that same day via a text message, which read: 'OK. £1,500. Just get it done on time.' Mr Aston replied: 'OK'. Mr Aston duly worked on the weekend days and finished the work on time.

Finn paid Aston £10,000 on the day the job was completed. Mr Aston then submitted a bill for the extra £1,500, but Mr Finn refused to pay it. Mr Finn has now found his copy of the contract (in an email archive) and it states that 'Saturday and Sunday shall both constitute working days for the purposes of this contract'.

Mr Aston sued to recover the extra £1,500 promised by Mr Finn. The Court of Appeal dismissed Mr Aston's appeal. Mr Aston now appeals, with leave, to the Supreme Court on the following grounds.

1. Mr Aston had provided consideration for the promise to pay the extra £1,500. Following the decision of the Court of Appeal in *Williams v Roffey Bros & Nicholls (Contractors) Ltd* **[1991] 1 QB 1**, Mr Finn obtained a practical benefit as a result of Mr Aston's promise to complete the work by Tuesday 22 May at 6pm.

2. The promise to pay the £1,500 had not been procured by the exercise of economic duress. Mr Aston had genuinely, albeit erroneously, believed that he was not required to work at the weekend. In the absence of bad faith on the part of Mr Aston, there was no basis for any conclusion that the promise to pay had been procured by the application of economic duress that was sufficient to set aside the promise to pay the £1,500: *CTN Cash and Carry Ltd v Gallaher Ltd* **[1994] 4 All ER 714**.

UNDERSTANDING THE BASICS OF THE PROBLEM QUESTION

Again we will begin by analysing the moot problem question. Below you will find a list of features identified by the relevant letter in the problem question above.

COURT
Aston v Finn is in the UK Supreme Court. The Supreme Court is neither bound by its previous decisions, nor those of any other court. However, *stare decisis* does operate here, which means that it has a system precedent with regard to its own decisions. This means that while it can change its previous decisions, it will not do so without significant justification.

APPELLANT
The first name indicates who is appealing to the appeal court. In this case, Les Aston is appealing the points of law to the Supreme Court after his initial appeal was rejected by the Court of Appeal (Civil Division).

RESPONDENT
The second name indicates who is responding to the appeal. In this case, Alfred Finn is responding to the appeal. In effect, the Respondent is asking the Supreme Court to affirm the Court of Appeal's decision.

D INCIDENT FACTS

The first four paragraphs set out the incident facts relevant to both grounds of appeal. It is worth noting that in this problem question, the incident facts cannot be easily divided by paragraph for each ground of appeal. The fact pattern as a whole relates to both grounds. This is important when the mooters come to selecting research terms.

E INITIAL CLAIM AND IMMEDIATE PROCEDURAL HISTORY

This explains the initial contractual claim that Aston filed against Finn. This paragraph also explains the procedural history and tells you what has happened in the court directly below the court in which the moot problem question is in. For example, the present case was last heard in the Court of Appeal.

F GROUND ONE OF THE APPEAL

This ground 'belongs' to Senior Counsel for both the Appellant and the Respondent, which in this case is Ali. The Appellant will argue for the appeal, whereas the Respondent will argue against. In **Aston v Finn**, the Senior Appellant will argue that Mr Aston should be able to recover the £1,500 because Mr Finn obtained a practical benefit from Mr Aston's promise to complete the work by Tuesday 22 May at 6pm. Note that the wording of the ground of appeal instructs the Senior Appellant to ask the Supreme Court to follow the case of *Williams v Roffey Bros & Nicholls (Contractors) Ltd* [1991] 1 QB 1. The Senior Respondent will argue the opposite to this, namely that Mr Aston should not be able to recover the £1,500. In doing so, the Senior Respondent may choose to ask the court to overrule *Williams v Roffey Bros*, distinguish it or choose not to follow it.

G GROUND TWO OF THE APPEAL

This ground 'belongs' to Junior Counsel for both the Appellant and the Respondent, which in this case is Anna. The Appellant will argue for the appeal, whereas the Respondent will argue against. In **Aston v Finn**, the Junior Appellant will argue that Mr Aston did not procure the £1,500 by economic duress. The Respondent will refute this. Note the case of *CTN Cash and Carry Ltd v Gallaher Ltd* [1994] 4 All ER 714 is cited but it does not instruct the mooters how to use it.

SUMMARISING THE CASE

We will now summarise the moot question in preparation for analysing the problem in more detail. This sub-section will begin with the summaries constructed by Ali and Anna. These summaries will form the basis for constructing a summary that is simultaneously concise and comprehensive.

Below are three variations of summaries. The first is from Ali, the second from Anna and the third is the one that we have constructed. You will see that all do summarise the fact pattern but you should compare and contrast them to look at which achieves this with the appropriate balance of detail and brevity.

- *Alfred Finn owns a block of ten apartments which he wants to rent out.*

- *In 2012 he arranged for a painter, Les Aston, to paint all the apartments before the tenants moved in.*

- *As per the contract, the work commenced on Monday 11 May 2012 and would take 15 days to complete. The fee was £10,000 payable in advance.*

- *A dispute arose when Aston refused to work weekends, saying he was not required to do so by the contract. Finn said that he was, but neither could find a copy of the contract.*

- *Finn had new tenants moving in on 23 May and so needed the work done by the evening of 22 May. This could only be done if Aston worked weekends.*

- *Eventually both men agreed that Aston would work weekends if Finn paid him an additional £1,500. Aston worked weekends and the work was completed on time.*

- *Finn found a copy of the contract, which stated that Aston was indeed required to work weekends. Finn refused to pay the extra £1,500 and Aston sued to recover it.*

- *Aston lost an appeal to the Court of Appeal and now appeals to the Supreme Court on the grounds that Aston had provided consideration for the £1,500 and Finn had obtained a practical benefit (Williams v Roffey Bros), and Aston had not used economic duress to get the extra £1,500 as he had genuinely believed he was not required to work weekends.*

Below is the summary constructed by Anna:

> *Finn is the owner of a block of ten luxury apartments. After having found tenants he made a contract with Mr Aston, a local painter, under which Mr Aston was to paint the apartments in 15 days. After having an argument about working at weekends and having not been able to find a copy of the contract, Finn agreed to pay an extra £1,500 for the work to be completed on time, provided Aston work at weekends. After the work was completed Finn refused to pay the amount as he had found the contract and it stated that Aston was to work at weekends. Aston is now appealing to the Supreme Court.*

Below is the summary we have constructed:

- *Finn contracted with Aston to paint a block of flats he owned.*

- *Finn needed the work completed by May 22, but Aston refused to work weekends, which jeopardised the work being completed on time. The two parties could not find a copy of the contract to clarify whether the contract included weekend work.*

- *To get the work completed on time, Finn agreed to pay an extra £1,500, after Aston threatened to have his team stop work. A copy of the contract later confirmed that weekend work had been expressly included within the contract. Finn refused to pay.*

- *Aston alleged breach of contract, and claimed for the extra £1,500. The Court of Appeal dismissed his claim. He now appeals to the Supreme Court, arguing that he provided consideration for the extra £1,500, and that it was not procured by economic duress.*

You will see that the summary we have constructed finds a balance between sufficient detail and brevity. This is a particularly difficult problem to achieve this with because the incident facts are quite detailed. However, by taking a focused approach, we achieve our aim. The first bullet point sets up the original contract, the second sets up the dispute, the third sets up the basis for the claim and the fourth shows how the claim has been dealt with so far by the courts, including the current grounds of appeal.

There are difficulties with each of the summaries. In Ali's summary, he includes superfluous detail, such as the number of apartments and all dates referenced. Anna, on the other hand, omits fundamentals, such as the current appeal points. With such a detailed set of facts, it is important to ensure that you filter out what is necessary, include what is fundamental and redraft to ensure a balance.

The key to drafting useful summaries is practice. Keeping in mind our guidance above, consider what you could edit out of Ali's summary below. To guide you, we have crossed out superfluous information contained in the first two bullet points.

- ~~Alfred~~ Finn owns a block of ~~ten~~ apartments ~~which he wants to rent out.~~

- ~~In 2012~~ he arranged for a painter, ~~Les~~ Aston, to paint ~~all~~ the apartments ~~before the tenants moved in.~~

- As per the contract, the work commenced on Monday 11 May 2012 and would take 15 days to complete. The fee was £10,000 payable in advance.

- A dispute arose when Aston refused to work weekends, saying he was not required to do so by the contract. Finn said that he was, but neither could find a copy of the contract.

- Finn had new tenants moving in on 23 May and so needed the work done by the evening of 22 May. This could only be done if Aston worked weekends.

- Eventually both men agreed that Aston would work weekends if Finn paid him an additional £1,500. Aston worked weekends and the work was completed on time.

- Finn found a copy of the contract, which stated that Aston was indeed required to work weekends. Finn refused to pay the extra £1,500 and Aston sued to recover it.

- Aston lost an appeal to the Court of Appeal and now appeals to the Supreme Court on the grounds that Aston had provided consideration for the £1,500 and Finn had obtained a practical benefit (Williams v Roffey Bros), and Aston had not used economic duress to get the extra £1,500 as he had genuinely believed he was not required to work weekends.

UNDERSTANDING YOUR GROUND OF APPEAL AND APPRECIATING WIDER LEGAL CONTEXT

The human rights law chapter underscored how important it is for advocates to read cases cited in the moot problem before going on to select research terms and undertake research. Carefully reading cases referenced in the moot problem will help you to better understand the wider legal context of the moot problem and the grounds of appeal, and assist you to select more useful research terms.

In **Aston v Finn**, two cases are referenced, respectively, in the first and second grounds of appeal, namely *Williams v Roffey Bros & Nicholls (Contractors) Ltd* [1991] 1 QB 1 and *CTN Cash and Carry Ltd v Gallaher Ltd* [1994] 4 All ER 714. These cases are available for free on the British and Irish Legal Information Institute (BAILII) website: www.bailii.org. You should read these cases before progressing further with this chapter.

This section summarises how the cases of *Williams* and *CTN* fit into the wider legal context of the grounds of appeal they relate to.

Ground One and *Williams*

Mr Aston had provided consideration for the promise to pay the extra £1,500. Following the decision of the Court of Appeal in *Williams v Roffey Bros & Nicholls (Contractors) Ltd* [1991] 1 QB 1, Mr Finn obtained a practical benefit as a result of Mr Aston's promise to complete the work by Tuesday 22 May at 6pm.

To be binding, a contract must be 'supported by consideration'. Consideration is thought of as 'the price of the promise', i.e. what one contracting party is getting, in return for his promise from the other. In the case of *Currie and others v Misa* (1874–1875) LR 10 Ex. 153, the court defined 'consideration' as '*either … some right, interest, profit, or benefit accruing to the one party, or some forbearance, detriment, loss, or responsibility, given, suffered, or undertaken by the other*'.

The concept of consideration is best considered by way of 'real life' examples. For example, David goes to the supermarket and buys bananas for £1. David gets the bananas and provides, by way of consideration, the price of £1. The store gets the £1 and, by way of consideration, provides the bananas in return. This is a classic simultaneous contract and performance.

In **Aston v Finn**, the original contract was for Aston to paint ten apartments in 15 days for the fee of £10,000. This is a classic bilateral contract, made before it is due to be performed. Finn's promise to pay the £10,000 is made in exchange for Aston's promise to paint the apartments. The disputed contract, however, namely Finn's promise to pay Aston an extra £1,500, is a unilateral contract. This is because Finn promised to pay the money if Aston performed a specific act, namely working weekends to finish the painting job. Here, Aston provides his consideration by doing the specified act, but Finn declines to provide his consideration, namely the extra £1,500. Hence, the dispute arises.

The case of *Williams* helps us to understand why the dispute arises legally. In that case, Roffey Bros, a building firm, had a contract to refurbish 27 flats and subcontracted the carpentry work to Williams for the price of £20,000. After finishing nine flats, Williams got into financial difficulties. Concerned they would be liable under a penalty clause in the main building contract if Williams did not complete the work on time, Roffey Bros agreed to pay Williams an extra £10,300. Williams completed eight more flats, but Roffey Bros only paid him an extra £1,500. Williams abandoned the job and Roffey Brothers incurred a penalty and had to engage new carpenters to complete the work. Williams sued Roffey Brothers claiming the outstanding balance for the work he completed. Roffey Brothers argued that Williams had provided no consideration for the additional promise they made. The Court of Appeal disagreed with Roffey Brothers, ruling there was consideration for the additional promise. In short, the consideration was the 'practical benefit' Roffey Brothers derived from Williams' subsequent performance.

On reading *Williams*, therefore, we can quickly see why the **Aston v Finn** moot problem references the *Williams* case in ground one of the appeal, and instructs the Senior Appellant to argue that the Supreme Court should follow the decision of the Court of Appeal in *Williams*.

The wider legal context of this ground of appeal is the concept of 'consideration'. Simply put, the Appellant will argue Aston did provide consideration in the form of a 'practical benefit' following *Williams*, and the Respondent will argue he didn't on the basis that *Williams* should be overruled or distinguished.

Williams, therefore, gives us at least four key research terms: 'consideration', 'practical benefit', 'additional promise' and 'unilateral contract'.

You will see these terms in the research section.

Ground Two and *CTN*

The promise to pay the £1,500 had not been procured by the exercise of economic duress. Mr Aston had genuinely, albeit erroneously, believed that he was not required to work at the weekend. In the absence of bad faith on the part of Mr Aston, there was no basis for any conclusion that the promise to pay had been procured by the application of economic duress that was sufficient to set aside the promise to pay the £1,500: *CTN Cash and Carry Ltd v Gallaher Ltd* [1994] 4 All ER 714.

The foundation of contract law lies in the concept of freedom of contract; each party to the contract should enter into the contract freely and of their own choice. Where a contract has been formed under duress, it can be vitiated. There are a number of forms of duress, one of which is economic duress, which forms the basis of this second ground of appeal.

Traditionally, there was no need for a principle of economic duress when determining the validity of contractual variations. This is because only variations supported by consideration were enforceable. In circumstances where unfair pressure was being exerted, it was highly likely that there was a lack of consideration and therefore no need for a concept of economic duress. Since the case of *Williams*, however, economic duress has developed to be of greater importance. The ruling in *Williams* allowed the enforceability of unilateral variations, which were absent traditional consideration. As a consequence, this case included the exception of economic duress to address situations of unfair economic pressure. This is not to say that if both parties provide consideration there cannot be a finding of economic duress. O'Sullivan and Hilliard (*The Law of Contract*, Oxford, Oxford University Press, 6th Edition, 2014) state that there are seemingly three distinct requirements for economic duress, namely:

(i) illegitimate pressure or threat
(ii) which, subjectively, caused the victim to act as he did,
(iii) which, objectively, would have caused a reasonable person in the victim's position to act in the same way.

From the case of *CTN*, we can figure out which of these elements is significant for the present ground of appeal in **Aston v Finn**. In *CTN*, the facts concern CTN, a cash and carry business, and Gallaher, a large business, which regularly sold cigarettes to CTN. Gallaher often provided CTN with significant credit, which CTN relied heavily upon. Gallaher had no contractual obligation to sell to CTN or to provide this credit. Gallaher sold a batch of cigarettes to CTN but delivered them to the incorrect address. Gallaher agreed to collect and redeliver the cigarettes but they were stolen before this could be done. Gallaher believed CTN was obliged to pay for the cigarettes and invoiced them for £17,000. When doing so, they made it clear they would not grant any more credit unless CTN paid. CTN did not believe they were obliged to pay but did so because of the threat to decline credit. CTN later attempted to reclaim the £17,000 on the ground that the threat to not provide credit amounted to economic duress. The Court of Appeal found that the threat did not amount to economic duress, stressing that Gallaher's good faith when the demand was made and the reasonable belief that they were entitled to be paid defeated the claim of economic duress.

On reading *CTN*, therefore, we can quickly see the relationship between the instant case and economic duress. **Aston v Finn**, and in particular this second ground, is concerned with the first element of economic duress, namely whether there existed an *illegitimate* pressure or threat. This requires a threat to breach an existing contract. It has also been found, however, that a threat may be illegitimate where it is one of lawful action.

In the instant case, the main issue is about the existence of good faith on the part of Aston; if his request for extra payment for weekend working was made in good faith then it would not be considered to be an illegitimate threat and economic duress would fail. However, sometimes a threat to do something lawful (such as not work weekends when you do not believe you are obliged to do so!) can amount to being illegitimate. In fact, there are a number of cases where it has been accepted that a threat may be illegitimate when coupled with a demand for payment even if the threat is one of lawful action.

CTN would therefore generate the following research terms: 'good faith', 'economic duress', 'genuine belief', 'reasonable belief' and 'entitled'.

You will see these terms utilised in the research section below.

The final stage for analysing the question is to ask yourself some simple questions to clarify your basic understanding of your ground of appeal:

- Am I arguing for the appeal to be allowed or dismissed?
- Am I arguing that Aston provided sufficient consideration for the variation of the contractual terms, or not?
- Am I arguing *Williams* should be followed, overruled or distinguished?
- Am I arguing that Aston's actions amounted to economic duress, or not?
- Am I arguing *CTN* should be followed, overruled or distinguished?

Once you are comfortable with the answers to these questions, you should be in a position to identify search terms that can be used to start your legal research.

RESEARCH

This section focuses on how to research the areas of law related to **Aston v Finn**.

Before going on to consider the specific research Ali and Anna undertook for this case, you should remind yourself of the preliminary considerations for researchers that we set out on page 14.

RESEARCHING ASTON V FINN

The rules in relation to **Aston v Finn** allowed Ali and Anna each to use three cases, any relevant legislation and two 'other' authorities, such as scholarship.

Below is a list of some of Ali and Anna's research terms:

Ali	Anna
contract	economic duress
consideration	pre-existing contract
existing duty	terms
benefit	new contract
detriment	
no benefit	

These research terms generated the following authorities:

Ali	Anna
• *Williams v Roffey Bros and Nicholls (Contractors) Ltd* [1991] 1 QB 1 • *Stilk v Myrick* [1809] 2 Camp 317 • *Ward v Byham* [1956] 1 WLR 496	• *Pao On v Lau Yiu Long* [1979] 3 All ER 65 • *North Ocean Shipping Co v Hyundai Constructors Co (The Atlantic Baron)* [1979] QB 705 • *Occidental Worldwide Investment Corporation v Skibs A/S Avanti (The Sibeon and The Sibotre)* [1976] 1 Lloyd's Rep. 293 • Richard Hooley, *Controlling contractual direction*, (2013) 72(1) CLJ 65 • Pinar Akman, *The relationship between economic duress and abuse of a dominant position*, (2014) 1 LMCLQ 99

There is no overlap in the cases or other authorities for each ground of appeal. This should not be taken as an excuse for not reviewing every authority chosen by the opposition. Sometimes, very helpful material can come from an unlikely source.

CASE SUMMARIES

The case summaries below are designed to show you how these cases address their relevant grounds of appeal.

Ground One

Authority	Summary	Relevance
Williams v Roffey Bros and Nicholls (Contractors) Ltd [1991] 1 QB 1	See page 128.	This is the main case that supports the Appellant's argument about there being valid consideration because the Respondent gained a benefit. The inclusion of this case is crucial because it is cited in the ground of appeal, and it is a leading case on consideration.
Stilk v Myrick [1809] 2 Camp 317	Stilk was a sailor who contracted with Myrick (a captain) to work on a ship sailing a return trip to the Baltic. During the voyage, two sailors deserted the ship and Myrick promised to divide the wages of the deserters to the rest of the crew (including Stilk) if they manned the ship for the return leg of the trip. On return to England, Myrick did not divide the additional wages as promised and Stilk alleged a breach of contract. The court rejected Stilk's claim; holding that because he provided no additional benefit to Myrick (he was contracted to sail the return ship anyway), there was no breach of contract.	The outcome of this case is in favour of the Respondent in **Aston v Finn**, as it provides an authority to argue that when someone completes a job they originally contracted to do, they provide no additional benefit that requires additional payment. Finn could use this case to argue that there was no consideration for the additional payment of £1,500 because Aston was simply performing his original obligations.

The Appellant would need to distinguish *Stilk*. They could do this in multiple ways. For example, argue the facts of *Stilk* are wholly irrelevant to **Aston v Finn**, or (drawing on the language of *Williams*) there was an additional practical benefit received by Finn in the instant case, unlike in *Stilk*.

Ward v Byham **[1956] 1 WLR 496**	Byham promised to pay Ward (the mother of his illegitimate child) £1 a week if she kept the child 'well and happy'. Byham stopped paying and Ward alleged a breach of contract. The Court of Appeal found in favour of Ward; holding that the promise to keep the child 'well and happy' was above the minimal level of care required and this was her consideration for the £1 weekly payment.	The Appellant could draw on this case to argue that sufficient consideration was provided by Aston because he went beyond his contractual requirements and worked weekends.
		The Respondent could, however, use *Ward* to argue that Aston did not exceed contractual obligations because the original contract when located confirmed that he was contractually obliged to work weekends.

Ground Two

Authority	**Summary**	**Relevance**
CTN Cash and Carry Ltd v Gallaher Ltd **[1994] 4 All ER 714**	See page 129.	This case relates to the second requirement for establishing economic duress, namely, did the threat cause the victim to act as he did. See pages 129–131 for a discussion of the second ground of appeal.

***Pao On v Lau Yiu Long* [1979] 3 All ER 65**

This case related to agreements dealing with the sale of shares between two companies. After entering into this agreement, the claimant realised that part of the deal was not advantageous. Consequently, they persuaded the other company to replace a subsidiary contract, saying that if this was not done then they would not proceed with the overall sale. The company agreed but subsequently sought to avoid liability under the contract, alleging *inter alia* that it was procured by economic duress. The Privy Council rejected the plea of economic duress.

Pao is not necessarily factually relevant to the current case, as it has such a specific fact pattern. In that case, however, Lord Scarman elaborated on factors to consider when assessing whether the threat caused the victim to act as he did and, consequently, whether economic duress could be found. Those factors are: (i) whether the victim protested; (ii) whether or not he had an alternative course available to him, such as an adequate legal remedy; (iii) whether or not the victim was independently advised; and (iv) whether or not, after entering the contract, he took steps to avoid it. Students would note through wider reading that these factors are not all equally weighted and are considered in some areas to be most relevant to the requirement of whether a reasonable person would act as the victim did.

***North Ocean Shipping Co v Hyundai Constructors Co (The Atlantic Baron)* [1979] QB 705**	This case dealt with a variation in price for the building of a ship. The court held that the demand for extra money did amount to economic duress but the fact that extra payments had been made without protest for several years amounted to an affirmation of the variation of the original contract. As such, there was not a successful plea of economic duress.	This case further considers the requirements for economic duress and demonstrates when such a plea will fail. The Appellant could utilise the principles discussed in *The Atlantic Baron* to argue that there had been no initial protest at the variation and, as such, this change had been affirmed by both parties. The Respondent, on the other hand, would argue that the lack of payment of any additional funds shows an attempt to avoid the contract and, consequently, shows economic duress.
***Occidental Worldwide Investment Corporation v Skibs A/S Avanti (The Sibeon and The Sibotre)* [1976] 1 Lloyd's Rep. 293**	This case dealt with a contract for ship hire. A subsequent agreement reduced the hire rate per month. The contentious issue was whether the subsequent agreement was induced by misrepresentation or made under duress. The claim for economic duress failed but this was the first case in English law to recognise that economic duress might vitiate a contract.	This case focuses upon the type of threat required for economic duress, namely, a threat must be 'illegitimate' (see above at page 131 for discussion of this). In *The Sibeon* case the court rejected the argument that any threat to breach a contract is automatically illegitimate. In the current case, the Appellant made a threat to breach the contract. Aston can use *The Sibeon* case as a starting point to argue that not every threat will form the platform for economic duress. The Respondent, however, will argue that the context of the threat made it illegitimate.

Richard Hooley, *Controlling contractual direction,* **(2013) 72(1) CLJ 65**	This article identifies what controls might be imposed by a court on the way a party exercises discretionary powers provided for under a contract. In particular, the article examines how 'good faith' plays a crucial role in this context.	This article could help the Appellant and Respondent to better grasp the concept of 'good faith' in contractual obligations. This would be useful for the second ground of appeal as 'good faith' can be relevant to assessing economic duress. Good faith is relevant to **Aston v Finn** because the Respondent could argue the Appellant acted in bad faith by erring about the original terms of the contract and taking advantage of the Respondent's need to have the work completed in a certain time frame.
Pinar Akman, *The relationship between economic duress and abuse of a dominant position,* **(2014) 1 LMCLQ 99**	This article compares the doctrine of economic duress with the concept of 'abuse of a dominant position' in competition law.	This article provides useful background reading for both the Appellant and the Respondent as it breaks down the doctrine of economic duress.

It is worth noting that there are a lot of cases that address consideration and economic duress across contract law. Mooters will need to filter these cases and choose those which best support their argument. The grounds of appeal do not make this easy for the mooter because they are drafted widely. For example, the second ground of appeal simply mentions economic duress and does not further narrow this to a particular requirement of economic duress. As such, knowing which authorities are the 'right' ones to choose can be difficult. The best approach in such a situation is to go for the simplest and most relevant argument. Also remember, that as a mooter, you are autonomous and can shape the argument in any way you choose. This can make for very interesting moots!

SUMMARY

This section has shown how research can be improved when you appreciate the wider legal context within which your argument falls.

ARGUMENT CONSTRUCTION

SUBMISSIONS FOR THE APPELLANT

This section will outline how Ali and Anna shaped submissions for the Appellant in a skeleton argument. Below is a copy of their first draft along with our feedback.

IN THE SUPREME COURT OF THE UNITED KINGDOM

Aston v Finn

Appellant's Skeleton Argument

Senior Counsel for the Appellant shall submit:

Ground One:

1. The Appellant's promise to work at weekends constitutes valid consideration because the Respondent gained a practical benefit and obviated a detriment as a result of the promise (*Williams v Roffey Bros and Nicholls (Contractors) Ltd* [1991] 1 QB 1).

This is a clearly drafted submission that zones in on the core of the Appellant's argument with regards to ground one of the appeal. The construction of the submission could be improved in order to gain greater effect, however. This can be done by using three shorter sentences. For instance, The Appellant's promise to work at weekends constitutes valid consideration. This is because the Respondent gained a practical benefit and obviated a detriment as a result of the promise. This court is urged to follow the ruling in **Williams v Roffey Bros and Nicholls (Contractors) Ltd** *[1991] 1 QB 1.*

2. Even if the Appellant was only offering to perform his existing obligations, this is still valid consideration as the agreement was instigated by the Respondent (*Ward v Byham* [1956] 1 WLR 496).

This submission is not clear. Ali is attempting to offer an alternative argument to the court should his first submission fail, but it is not clear how he plans to use Ward as an authority for this. He needs to more precisely link the ruling in Ward to the facts of Aston v Finn.

3. Dismissing this appeal would result in a binding miscarriage of justice, because it would mean that contractual promises in this area of the law

would no longer be legally enforceable. Allowing this appeal would help to clarify and modernise the legal position in this area, as the case of **Stilk v Myrick** is outdated and fails to take into account the agreement made by the parties involved.

The second sentence of the submission is acceptable, although Ali wrongly omits to use a full case citation for Stilk and could use more precise language. However, his first sentence is distractingly vague and without clear meaning. It appears Ali is trying to suggest that if the appeal fails the court would be encouraging breach of contract in cases such as Aston v Finn (which are not uncommon contractual relationships); however, this is not suggested in a sophisticated way.

Junior Counsel for the Appellant shall submit:

Ground Two:

1. There was a genuine belief by the Appellant for his actions and therefore the absence of bad faith shows no evidence of economic duress, in contrast to the case of **Occidental Worldwide Investment Corporation v Skibs A/S Avanti (The Sibeon and The Sibotre) [1976] 1 Lloyd's Rep. 293. CTN Cash and Carry Ltd. v Gallaher Ltd (1994) 4 All ER 714.**

Anna is trying to underscore that the Appellant did not act in bad faith and a plea of economic duress should therefore fail. She does not make this argument clearly in respect of the construction of her sentences or the use of her authorities, however. For example, there is no indication of how she wishes the court to utilise (if at all) the CTN case.

2. The Respondent was aware and took advantage of the situation as he gained a benefit by paying the additional sum similarly to the case of **Pao On v Lau Yiu Long (1979) 3 All ER 65.**

This submission is confused. Anna uses an authority relevant to economic duress, but seems to overstep into the realms of ground one by making comment about 'gaining a benefit'. Anna needed to focus more closely on the requirements of economic duress and how the factors highlighted in Pao inform that assessment.

3. Disallowing this appeal would over broaden economic duress.

This is an acceptable argument, but Anna's submission requires expansion and authority. At very least, she needs to provide a reason 'why' disallowing the appeal would have this effect.

SUBMISSIONS FOR THE RESPONDENT

On page 141 we have used Ali and Anna's research for the Respondent to construct submissions for the Respondent. Contrast our skeleton argument with the draft Appellant skeleton argument above. Generally, we have attempted to be as precise as possible when linking the instant case facts to relevant law and outline our arguments clearly. We also make it clear how we wish the presiding court to consider the authorities we cite. The presentation of our submissions is also consistent and 'tidy'. For ground one, we have focused on how the Respondent wants the court to consider the cases of *Williams, Stilk and Ward*, and how those cases support the argument that there was no consideration for the additional payment of £1,500. For ground two, we have built our submissions around the requirements for economic duress.

IN THE SUPREME COURT OF THE UNITED KINGDOM

Aston v. Finn

Respondent's Skeleton Argument

Senior Counsel for the Respondent shall submit:

Ground One:

1. The Respondent's agreement to pay the extra £1,500 is not supported by consideration. This is because the Respondent gained no additional benefit from the Appellant working weekends as this was a requirement of the original contract. The case of *Williams v Roffey Bros and Nicholls (Contractors) Ltd* [1991] 1 QB 1 is distinguishable.

2. The Appellant was already contractually obliged to work weekends as per the original contract. As such, there is no valid consideration for the extra £1,500 payment because the Appellant was already obliged to perform the duties he was offering, following *Stilk v Myrick* [1809] 2 Camp 317. The case of *Ward v Byham* [1956] 1 WLR 496 is distinguishable because the Appellant did not exceed any of his original obligations.

3. Allowing this appeal would unfairly over-broaden the 'practical benefit' principle established in *Williams*. The Respondent urges this court to affirm the principle in *Stilk* and confine *Williams* to its facts. In so ruling, the court will deter contractors from demanding extra payments for work they are already contractually obliged to complete.

Junior Counsel for the Respondent shall submit:

Ground Two:

1. The instant case meets the requirements for a plea of economic duress. The Appellant made an illegitimate threat to the Respondent by coupling his demand for additional payment with the statement that he would direct his employees to immediately stop work. This illegitimate threat caused the Respondent to act as he did and agree to pay the additional £1,500. A reasonable person would have acted in the same way. See *Pao On v Lau Yiu Long* (1979) 3 All ER 65.

2. The Respondent both protested against providing additional payment and took immediate steps to avoid the contract. These

actions are indicative of economic duress. See ***Pao On***. In particular, following ***North Ocean Shipping Co v Hyundai Constructors Co (The Atlantic Baron)* [1979] QB 705**, non-payment of additional monies is indicative of economic duress.

3. The Respondent was not in a comparable bargaining position to the Appellant, unlike in the case of ***Pao On*** where economic duress failed. The Appellant took advantage of the Respondent's need to have the work completed by a certain deadline and thus acted in bad faith, following ***CTN Cash and Carry Ltd v Gallaher Ltd* [1994] 4 All ER 714**. Allowing this appeal would encourage such exploitation.

THINKING AHEAD AND BEING CRITICAL

Once your submissions are drafted, you must start to think critically about your argument. This involves thinking ahead to what sorts of questions the judge might ask you during the course of your moot. The two concepts are closely related because the judge will seek to clarify and test your arguments.

General questions about each ground of appeal

This section considers some general questions a judge could ask the advocates about this appeal. These questions are designed to get you thinking about both some of the broader legal concepts related to this appeal and how certain facts could be of concern to a judge. For each question, we provide some guidance on giving an appropriate answer from both the Appellant and the Respondent's perspective.

Ground One

● *What are the requirements of a valid contract?*

Guidance: *This is a general question that would require the same answer for both the Appellant and the Respondent. This question is testing the mooter's wider knowledge. A good answer would set out the requirements for a valid contract in a simple list format. These are, in basic terms, an intention to create legal obligations, offer and acceptance, consideration and capacity. It would be good practice for a mooter to then highlight which requirement – i.e. consideration – is at issue in the instant case.*

- *What is consideration?*

Guidance: *This is a general question that would require the same answer for both the Appellant and the Respondent. A good answer will not only acknowledge the complexity of consideration as a legal concept, but also explain it clearly in its most basic form. A basic explanation of 'consideration' can be found on page 128. Once a mooter has explained the concept of consideration in terms of 'benefits' and 'detriment', it would be good practice to link it to the instant case in favour of their client. For example, the Appellant would make the point that the Respondent received a benefit by the Appellant working weekends, whereas the Respondent would challenge that point.*

- *How does a practical benefit form sufficient consideration?*

Guidance: *This is a general question that would require the same answer for both the Appellant and the Respondent, to the extent they would both need to explain that the law has determined that a 'practical benefit' can be sufficient consideration. The Appellant would then make the point that such a benefit exists in the instant case, whereas the Respondent would oppose that argument. A good way to explain what a practical benefit is, in terms of consideration, would be to use the explanation provided in the* Williams *case. This would not only help the mooter to be accurate but also showcase for the judge their detailed knowledge of the case law.*

- *Do the facts of the instant case reflect those of Williams?*

Guidance: *Both the Appellant and the Respondent should be ready to dissect the case of* Williams *for ground one of the appeal. In answering this question, the Appellant should focus on how the* Williams *case is similar to the instant case, whereas the Respondent should focus on how the cases differ.*

- *Is the fact that the original contract did require weekend work crucial to this case?*

Guidance: *The Appellant would need to answer this question in a way that dilutes the importance of this fact, and reroute the judge's attention to the fact that the Appellant genuinely believed weekend work was not included in the original contract. The Respondent, however, should seek to capitalise on the judge's interest in this fact and demonstrate how this fact cannot be ignored, not only because to do so would be unfair, but also because it has not been ignored in previous case law, such as* Stilk.

Ground Two

- *What does the phrase 'vitiate a contract' mean?*

Guidance: *This is a general question that would require the same answer for both the Appellant and the Respondent with regards to the definition of the phrase. To vitiate a contract simply means to make it legally invalid. The Appellant would then make the point that economic duress is not present to vitiate the contract for the £1,500, whereas the Respondent will make the point it is.*

- *What are the requirements for a plea of economic duress?*

Guidance: *This is a general question that would require the same answer for both the Appellant and the Respondent. A good answer will both acknowledge the complexity of economic duress as a legal concept, but also explain it clearly in its most basic form. A basic explanation of economic duress can be found on page 130. After providing an explanation, it would be good practice for the Appellant and Respondent to draw the court's attention to their arguments concerning each requirement.*

- *Do the facts of the instant case reflect those of CTN?*

Guidance: *Both the Appellant and the Respondent should be ready to dissect the case of CTN for ground two of the appeal. In answering this question, the Appellant could focus on how the bad faith present in CTN is not present in the instant case because the Appellant genuinely believed he was not contracted to work weekends, whereas the Respondent could focus on how bad faith is evidenced by the Appellant's exploitation of the Respondent's need to have the work completed by a certain deadline, which could only be achieved by the Appellant working weekends.*

- *Are all threats to breach a contract illegitimate?*

Guidance: *To answer this question, both the Appellant and the Respondent could direct the judge to the Sibeon case, where the court clearly stated that not all threats to breach a contract are considered illegitimate for the purposes of economic duress. The Appellant would then make the point that, although the Appellant did make a threat to stop working, the context of the threat (i.e. his genuine belief weekend work was not included in the contract) meant that it was not illegitimate. The Respondent, of course, would argue that the context of the original contract actually requiring weekend work means the threat was illegitimate.*

- *Would it make any difference if, hypothetically, the Respondent could have engaged new painters?*

Guidance: This question is really asking whether or not the Respondent could have engaged new painters. The answer for both the Appellant and the Respondent to this question is that, yes, theoretically, the Respondent could have at least tried to engage new painters. However, both advocates might be best served to redirect the judge away from this point. This is because the question whether new painters could be engaged or not is irrelevant to the instant appeal. This is because of the simple fact the Respondent did not engage new painters and the instant appeal involves a dispute between these two parties. The Respondent, however, could use this question to direct the judge's attention to how the Respondent did not have a lot of time to get the work done because he had made arrangements for tenants to move into the flats. This point would go directly towards the Respondent's third submission about the Appellant's exploitation of the situation.

Generally, however, when faced with a hypothetical question from a judge, a useful tactic is to underscore the hypothetical situation is not before the court instantly.

SUMMARY

It is always important for mooters to be familiar with the broader legal concepts relevant to their ground of appeal. It is also important that they have a detailed knowledge of the cases cited in the moot problem question and in the skeleton arguments, so they are able to make use of the cases to answer judicial questions. Mooters should also spend time anticipating what questions a judge might ask about specific facts in the case, or any hypothetical scenarios the judge might ask the mooter to consider.

CONCLUSION

In this chapter, we have shown you how to analyse, research and construct an argument in relation to the moot problem presented by the fictitious case of **Aston v Finn.**

5 LAW OF EQUITY

INTRODUCTION

In this chapter, we show you how to analyse, research and construct an argument in relation to the moot problem presented by the fictitious case of **Murray v Jokker**. This is an equity themed moot problem question.

This chapter takes a different format. This chapter aims to help you put into practice the lessons learned in previous chapters. We will guide you through the sections of analysis, research and argument construction, as in previous chapters, but this time you, the reader, will take the place of Ali and Anna in working through the stages alongside us. To that end, there are dedicated workspaces for you to undertake certain tasks throughout the course of this chapter.

ANALYSIS

THE PROBLEM QUESTION

A IN THE SUPREME COURT OF THE UNITED KINGDOM

MURRAY **B**

V

JOKKER **C**

D When Elizabeth Murray was 19, she started a relationship with a 38-year-old businessman, Phillip Jokker. At that time, Phillip owned a large Georgian house, which he had bought for £270,000. Two years afterwards, Elizabeth graduated with a first class medicine degree and had ambitions to become a surgeon. That summer, she moved into Phillip's house and ran the household for them both while Phillip carried on working. Elizabeth did not become a surgeon; instead, she and Philip had a child, Isla, and Elizabeth looked after the house.

After a few years, Elizabeth asked Phillip whether they could buy a new house and share the ownership. Phillip said that he couldn't imagine selling the Georgian house but repeatedly told Elizabeth that the house was theirs and was as much hers as it was his. When Elizabeth was 30, she received a large sum of inheritance, which she used to convert the cellar of the house into a lavish office and gym for Phillip. The conversion increased the value of the house by 20 per cent.

Phillip and Elizabeth have recently separated and Elizabeth has moved into a rented house with Isla. Phillip has paid off his £170,000 mortgage and the house is now worth £356,000.

Elizabeth brought proceedings in the Chancery Division of the High Court for 50 per cent of the value of the Georgian house, relying on the combined effect of the House of Lords rulings in **_Lloyds Bank Plc v Rosset_ [1991] AC 107** and **_Stack v Dowden_ [2007] UKHL 17**.

In the High Court Parity J found:

E 1. There was no initial acquisition of property by Elizabeth and therefore the judges were unable to find an imputed common intention to share the beneficial interest (**_Jones v Kernott_ [2011] UKSC 53**).

2. Lord Neuberger in **_Stack v Dowden_** allowed for an imputed intention to be objectively deduced from what the parties, as 'reasonable and just people', would have thought at the relevant time having regard to the

148

whole course of dealing between them to achieve a fair and just solution. Awarding 50 per cent of the value of the house would be unfair and unjust and Elizabeth was instead awarded 20 per cent (£71,200).

The Court of Appeal unanimously upheld the judgment of Parity J. Elizabeth is now appealing to the Supreme Court on the following grounds:

F 1. The court should apply the decision in *Jones v Kernott* that unanimously accepted the notion of imputing an intention of what the parties must have intended by reference to a yardstick of fairness, without an initial acquisition of beneficial interest.

G 2. It is open to the court to impute an intention as to the size of the party's respective interests and in this case a 50 per cent equitable interest is fair.

UNDERSTANDING THE BASICS OF THE PROBLEM QUESTION

You will remember from previous chapters that the best place to begin with a moot is by ensuring that you fully understand the moot problem question. This is best done by breaking up the problem question and ensuring that you understand all the different parts. Read the problem question above and see whether you are able to explain what letters A–G represent. Jot your answers down using the table below. Once you have done this, turn over to our explanation and compare it with your own.

A	
B	
C	
D	
E	
F	
G	

A COURT

Murray v Jokker is in the UK Supreme Court. Remember that this is important to note in terms of precedent and authority. While the Supreme Court is not formally bound by its previous decisions or those of any other court, *stare decisis* does operate here. This means that it does operate a system of precedent with regard to its own decisions; while it can change its previous decisions, it will not do so without significant justification.

B APPELLANT

The Appellant here is Elizabeth Murray. She will be appealing the points of law to the Supreme Court after her appeal at the Court of Appeal was rejected.

C RESPONDENT

The Respondent here is Philip Jokker. He will be responding to the appeal points raised in the grounds of appeal.

D INCIDENT FACTS

The first three paragraphs set out the incident facts relevant to both grounds of appeal. This is a slightly complex problem and the incident facts are quite detailed. Ensure that you understand the sequence of events here.

E INITIAL CLAIM AND IMMEDIATE PROCEDURAL HISTORY

This explains the initial claim made by Murray against Jokker in the High Court. It also explains the precise legal findings of that court, as well as the outcome and findings of the Court of Appeal. This is important for understanding the points of law at play in the instant appeal, and for giving some initial direction to your research.

F GROUND ONE OF THE APPEAL

This ground 'belongs' to Senior Counsel for both the Appellant and the Respondent. The Appellant will be arguing that the appeal should be allowed and the Respondent will be arguing that it should be dismissed. This ground of appeal has a number of detailed legal principles in it, as well as a specific case citation. This citation provides you with an initial point for research. The Appellant should be arguing that *Jones v Kernott* should be applied instantly, and, with reference to the principle of fairness, the court can impute an intention, meaning they can 'find' an intention to share ownership. The Respondent will need to make an argument that this case is either not followed or is distinguished.

G **GROUND TWO OF THE APPEAL**

This ground 'belongs' to Junior Counsel for both the Appellant and the Respondent. The Appellant will be arguing that the appeal should be allowed and the Respondent will be arguing that it should be dismissed. The second ground is strongly linked to the first with a focus on what the principle of fairness means. The Appellant will be arguing that the court is open to utilise fairness as a principle, and that this should mean a division of 50 per cent each between the parties. The Respondent will be arguing that this is not the case.

SUMMARISING THE CASE

Once you are sure that you understand the problem question and its different elements, then you can move on to the next stage: summarising the question. Remember the key elements for developing a good summary set out on pages 90–91.

With these in mind, construct a summary for **Murray v Jokker** below. Your summary should comprise five key points, plus information about the current appeal.

Once you have constructed your summary, compare it to the summary we constructed on the following page.

Summary of Murray v Jokker

- Murray and Jokker are an unmarried couple who recently separated.

- During the relationship they lived in a home that Jokker had purchased, for which after a while Murray gave money to pay for improvements.

- Murray had originally planned a medical career but did not pursue this, instead looking after the home and their child.

- Having recently separated, Murray is now pursuing a claim for half the value of the family home, which was rejected by the High Court and Court of Appeal.

- Murray now appeals to the Supreme Court. First, on the basis that the decision in Jones v Kernott accepted that imputing an intention must be done by reference to a yardstick of fairness. Second, that the Court has the power to impute an intention as to the size of respective interests and, in this case, a 50 per cent interest is fair.

You will see that the summary we have constructed finds a balance between sufficient detail and brevity.

UNDERSTANDING YOUR GROUND OF APPEAL AND APPRECIATING WIDER LEGAL CONTEXT

The previous chapters have sought to outline the importance in understanding your ground of appeal and doing sufficient reading prior to selecting research terms and fully engaging in your research.

The grounds of appeal in **Murray v Jokker** are as follows:

Ground One

The court should apply the decision in *Jones v Kernott* that unanimously accepted the notion of imputing an intention of what the parties must have intended by reference to a yardstick of fairness, without an initial acquisition of beneficial interest.

Ground Two

It is open to the court to impute an intention as to the size of the party's respective interests and in this case a 50 per cent equitable interest is fair.

Understanding the Wider Legal Context

In addition to generally understanding the position you must take on your ground of appeal, you must appreciate the wider legal context of the topic area. We underscored this fact in relation to secondary victims in the tort law chapter, consideration and economic duress in the contract law chapter and European and domestic human rights frameworks in the human rights law chapter. You should revisit those chapters to remind yourself how we did this.

To prepare for your moot in **Murray v Jokker** you should consider doing some general reading from a good-quality textbook on the basis of equity as an area of law. This will make your more detailed research more straightforward. It is also worth noting that there is a case cited in the first ground of appeal and that other cases are mentioned in the moot problem. You will remember from previous chapters that we recommend reading these cases, in full, at this stage.

Once you have undertaken this initial reading, you should be able to answer the questions in the box below. We have provided a space for you to jot down your answers. Once completed, you should compare your answers to ours on the following page.

What is equity?

What is a trust?

What is an 'equitable interest'?

What is a 'constructive trust'?

What is a 'resulting trust'?

Below are *very brief and basic* answers to the above questions so that you can check your understanding. Remember that our points here are only very brief and exist for the purpose of you checking whether you are going in the right direction.

What is 'equity'?
It is difficult to provide a definition with any great certainty but equity is a long-standing area of English law. It was developed by the courts to enable fairness to be provided in the case law. The principles of equity are now largely focused upon the development of trusts as an area of law.

What is a 'trust'?
A trust is essentially a legal relationship. It allows property to be held by some people (trustees) but for the benefit of other people (beneficiaries). It is possible for trustees to also be beneficiaries. There are different types of trusts and they can form in a number of ways.

What is an 'equitable interest'?
This is held by beneficiaries to a trust; beneficiaries have an 'interest' in the property held on trust and it is this interest that gives them rights.

What is a 'constructive trust'?
Constructive trusts are not deliberately created but rather are imposed by the court in certain circumstances. These trusts are usually imposed when someone has wrongfully acquired the property of another and fairness requires that the person who has been 'wronged' gains an interest in the trust property.

What is a 'resulting trust'?
Resulting trusts are not deliberately created. The trust is created by law because of certain circumstances that exist. There are two main types of resulting trust: automatic and presumed. The idea of a resulting trust is that the trust property returns, or 'results back', to its rightful owner.

Understanding Your Ground of Appeal

Once you are clear on the answers to the above questions, you can engage in the final stage of analysing the question: check your understanding of your ground of appeal. To do this, ask yourself some simple questions:

- Am I arguing for the appeal to be allowed or dismissed?
- Am I arguing that *Jones v Kernott* should be applied, followed, distinguished or overruled?
- Am I arguing that this court has the authority to impute an intention as to the size of each party's respective interests?
- Am I arguing that a 50 per cent equitable interest would be fair or unfair?

Once you are comfortable with the answers to these questions, you should be in a position to identify search terms that can be used to start your legal research.

RESEARCH

This section focuses on how to research the areas of law related to **Murray v Jokker**. Note the rules allow you to select three cases, any relevant legislation and two 'other' sources.

GENERATING RESEARCH TERMS

Your next task is to begin developing research terms for the moot problem. Before doing so, remind yourself of the preliminary considerations for researchers that we set out on page 14.

Once you are clear on those considerations, you should begin to develop your research terms. You should begin by looking at the moot problem and consider what 'obvious' words or terms you think are important for each ground of appeal. These terms will come from any point in the problem, not just from the grounds themselves; all of the facts have been included for some reason. Look through the problem and think about what words point to significant facts in the question. You should also further refine your terms once you have done some initial reading in the area, by developing 'hidden' terms. This initial reading will lead you to more 'legal' terms to include in your research. You may also want to include useful synonyms. You should use the box below to develop a list of research terms for each ground of appeal.

Ground One	Ground Two

Once you have selected your research terms, compare and contrast them with the terms below that we have developed. It is important to remember that there is no 'right' answer here. If your terms differ to the ones below, this does not mean that they are wrong. Look at any differences and think about why we have selected ours and why you have selected yours.

Ground One	Ground Two
impute an intention	impute an intention
yardstick of fairness	respective interests
Jones v Kernott	quantification
intention	equitable interest
beneficial interest	50 per cent
acquisition of beneficial interest	the house was theirs
looked after the house	inheritance
relationship	increased the value
the house was theirs	
inheritance	

GENERATING AUTHORITIES

Once you have identified your research terms, you should undertake your paper or electronic legal research. Remember to keep a research trail as you go. Examples of research trails can be found in the criminal law and tort law chapters. Generate a list of useful authorities for your ground of appeal as you undertake this process. You can list your chosen authorities in the box below.

Ground One	Ground Two

In utilising our research terms on online legal research databases, we generated the following sources. Consider whether these differ at all to those that you have come across.

Ground One	Ground Two
• *Jones v Kernott* [2011] UKSC 53 • *Westdeutsche Landesbank Girozentrale v Islington London BC* [1996] AC 669 • *Paragon Finance Plc v DB Thakerar & Co* [1999] 1 All ER 400 • *Lloyds Bank Plc v Rosset* [1991] AC 107	• *Midland Bank Plc v Cooke* [1995] 4 All ER 562 • *Oxley v Hiscock* [2005] Fam 211 • *Stack v Dowden* [2007] UKHL 17 • Cohabitation: The Financial Consequences of Relationship Breakdown, Law Com No. 307 • Sharing Homes: A Discussion Paper, Law Com. 278

SUMMARISING THE RELEVANCE OF YOUR AUTHORITIES

The case summaries below further explain our choice of cases. This should provide some assistance to you in two main ways:

1. If you have selected different sources, it will explain to you why we made the choices that we did.
2. If you selected the same sources, it will allow you to see whether you had the same rationale as us.

Ground One

Source   ***Jones v Kernott* [2011] UKSC 53**

Summary   Ms Jones was a mobile hairdresser and Mr Kernott was a self-employed ice cream salesman. J bought a mobile home which K later moved into. They then bought a property in joint names which had a low purchase price (£30,000) as it belonged to a relative of J. The property was funded by £6,000 cash from J and the remainder from an endowment mortgage in joint names. K contributed £100 a week to household expenses with the remainder coming from J. A joint loan was taken out by the couple to extend the property with K and friends doing the work. This increased the value of the property by 50 per cent. K left the family home and for the following 14 years all expenses ere met by J, including the majority of expenses for raising children. A joint insurance policy was later cashed in to allow K to put down a deposit on his own home. When J came to sell, K claimed an equitable interest. The Supreme Court found a division of 90/10 in favour of J. This was broadly reflective of financial contributions to the property with little else having any meaningful impact.

Relevance to the Grounds of Appeal   First and foremost, this case is referenced in the ground of appeal. As such, it should be thoroughly researched and understood by the mooter. This case shows that the presumption is that the names on the legal title should be definitive. This can, however, be rebutted by showing

(a) different common intention at the time the home was acquired, or (b) a later common intention formed showing the shares would change. This common intention is to be deduced objectively from conduct. This objective deduction should be made with considerations of fairness and with regard to the whole course of dealing.

The Appellant would, therefore, use this case to argue that fairness would require an imputed intention of shared equitable interest. As each case will turn on its facts, they will need to use the moot problem facts to make this argument.

The Respondent will argue that there was no change of the original intention and that the interests of fairness do not require this.

Source	***Westdeutsche Landesbank Girozentrale v Islington London BC* [1996] AC 669**
Summary	This case has a complex set of facts. The parties in this case were engaged in a ten-year agreement on interest rate swaps based on a notional sum of £25 million. There was also payment of an initial lump sum and under the agreement the council should have made a number of interest payments. The council stopped making payments and the bank brought an action for payment of the balance plus interest. It was held that the bank should recover some simple interest payments. The court made this determination using the concept of the resulting trust.
Relevance to the Grounds of Appeal	Constructive trusts (and resulting trusts) would be enforced on the grounds of conscience. Enforcement will arise where it would be unconscionable for the legal owner to deny a beneficial interest to the person claiming it.

This case can generally be used by the Appellant in arguing that it would be unconscionable not to impose a constructive trust and by the Respondent in generally arguing that it would not be unconscionable to refuse a trust. The intentions of the parties do not give rise to this. The advocates here should look at the financial relationship between Jokker and Murray, as well as conversations – for example, what was meant by the house being 'as much hers as it was his'. They may also look at the way in which the relationship worked; whether both parties considered themselves to be in a relationship that sought to share equally.

Source

***Paragon Finance Plc v DB Thakerar & Co* [1999] 1 All ER 400**

Summary

P were mortgage lenders who had lent money for the purchase of flats. T was a firm of solicitors who acted for P and the purchasers. It was discovered that the flats had been purchased at an inflated price and P lost money. P sued for breach of contract and breach of fiduciary duty as they had similar duties to trustees. The court made a number of distinctions about types of trusts.

Relevance to the Grounds of Appeal

Lord Justice Millett explained the two types of constructive trust:

'*A constructive trust arises by operation of law whenever the circumstances are such that it would be unconscionable for the owner of property (usually but not necessarily the legal estate) to assert his own beneficial interest in the property and deny the beneficial interest of another.*'

It determined that one case of constructive trust will be in the case of fraud and the other will be where a trust is intended from the outset and to refuse another their beneficial interest would be unconscionable.

Generally, this case only has relevance for the general concept of constructive trusts as the particular facts focus upon the fraud cases.

Source	*Lloyds Bank Plc v Rosset* [1991] AC 107
Summary	H acquired a semi-derelict farmhouse, which he planned to renovate together with W in order for it to become the family home. W oversaw all building work and believed that it had been acquired without a mortgage. H acquired a mortgage and fell into arrears. The bank sought repossession in lieu of payment and W sought to resist on the basis of an equitable interest which was overriding due to her occupation of the property. The House of Lords held that supervising building work was too peripheral to acquire an equitable interest.
Relevance to the Grounds of Appeal	Established that the basis on which a common intention constructive trust would be formed was twofold:

(i) Common intention based on conduct.

(ii) Common intention based on agreement.

In this problem we are largely concerned with (i). The significant discussion from Lord Bridge is that he largely conceives of such conduct in being direct contributions to the purchase price, either at the time of purchase or later through contributions to mortgage payments.

This would clearly favour the Respondent's argument.

Ground Two

Source	**Law Commission, Cohabitation: The Financial Consequences of Relationship Breakdown, Law Com No. 307**
Summary	This report looks at the legal and financial consequences for cohabitees when relationships break down. The Law Commission propose legal reform and a statutory scheme to regulate the separation of cohabitees.
Relevance to the Grounds of Appeal	The Appellant can utilise this report and its recognition of the changing demographics in England and Wales to argue that the law needs reform in this area. The moot problem shows a cohabiting couple and the difficulties that arise when a relationship breaks down. The Appellant could argue that the law in this area is out of date and needs reform to better address such relationships.

161

Source   ***Stack v Dowden* [2007] UKHL 17**

Summary   H and W were in a long-term relationship. Throughout this relationship, however, they kept all financial affairs separate. W bought the couple's first home and it was placed solely in her name. The second family home was bought using funds divided up 65 per cent cash from W and a 35 per cent mortgage taken out by H. When an action was brought considering the division of ownership of this property, the Court of Appeal held that the contributions should be divided 65 per cent/35 per cent in favour of W to reflect their respective financial contributions. This was in spite of a statement to the effect that the parties should be beneficial owners in equal shares. This was upheld by the House of Lords but with slightly different reasoning. The House held that the persons listed on the legal title would always be presumed to be the owners of the legal interest, whether one person or two and irrespective of any other persons involvement. This was, however, simply a presumption and one that could be rebutted.

Relevance to the Grounds of Appeal   It established the following key principles:

(i) Where there is an express trust then that express trust will be decisive of the parties' equitable interests.

(ii) If the legal title of the property is held by only one person there is a presumption that they will hold the equitable interest. If the legal title is held by two people then the presumption will be that they will both hold the equitable interest.

(iii) Where someone is seeking to claim a beneficial interest where the legal title is held by one person then the burden will rest on them to prove an interest.

This case is a foundational one. The Appellant would use it to argue that any presumption of interest on the part of Jokker can be rebutted and should be. The Respondent should use this to argue that the presumption of interest should not be rebutted.

It also gives a method for quantifying interest if one is to be implied.

Source	***Oxley v Hiscock* [2005] Fam 211**
Summary	Hiscock and Oxley purchased a house using £60,000 from Hiscock and £36,000 from Oxley; she also had further outgoings. The court focused on this and divided the equitable interest 60 per cent/40 per cent in favour of Hiscock.
Relevance to the Grounds of Appeal	The court attempted to review the case law in this area. The court held that they should first look for an agreement in the area and then, only in the absence of such an agreement, look at the 'whole course of dealing'. The Appellant could use this to argue that the whole course of dealing between the parties shows an equal division. The Respondent, on the other hand, would argue that when considering the interest of each of the parties this does not show a 50/50 division.
Source	***Midland Bank Plc v Cooke* [1995] 4 All ER 562**
Summary	H and W purchased a property for £8,500, the title of which was solely in H's name. This was done as follows:

£6,450 (mortgage)
£1,100 (wedding gift)
£950 (H cash)

The initial mortgage was later replaced by a more general one which allowed H to pay off the company's business overdraft. W later signed a consent form to subordinate any interest in the bank's mortgage. The bank later sought forfeiture and possession of the house in default of payment and W claimed undue influence and an equitable interest in the house. The court took a broader approach than the strictly mathematical one seen before: the couple 'had agreed to share everything equally'.

Relevance to the Grounds of Appeal	This case gives a method for quantifying interest. While previous cases had focused on contributions made to address the quantification of interest, this case utilised a broader concept of the whole course of dealing. The agreement between the couple to share everything equally was reflected in a 50 per cent division between the parties. The Appellant could use this case to argue that a 50 per cent division should be accepted as the intention between the parties was to share their lives equally. The Respondent could use this case to argue that there was no such intention and that 50 per cent would not be an appropriate share that reflected the whole course of dealing between the parties.
Source	**Law Commission, Sharing Homes: A Discussion Paper, Law Com. 278**
Summary	This paper sought to look at the question of people buying homes together and, in particular, to consider the legal issues arising when homes are bought collectively by individuals and no express arrangements are made for the division of ownership of the property. The paper sought to address the question of when an individual will gain a share in a property and what quantity that share will be. The paper argues that a statutory approach would be inappropriate and that the law should encourage formalisation of ownership in legal title and take a 'contributions-based' approach to assessing and quantifying shares in property.
Relevance to the Grounds of Appeal	After a detailed analysis, the Law Commission's conclusion in this paper is that developing a statutory scheme for all relationships that may be encountered in property ownership is not feasible. As such, this can be used by the Respondent to argue that the current legal framework is acceptable as it stands. Individuals should be encouraged to formalise their ownership arrangements through legal title and any exceptions should be dealt with using a contributions-based approach.

The above cases are simply the ones that our research led us to. It is entirely possible that in your research you may have encountered, and selected, different sources. If that is the case, before moving on to constructing an argument, you should now attempt to summarise the facts of your chosen authorities and their relevance to the grounds of appeal. You can create summary tables like the ones above to do this.

SUMMARY

This section has shown how straightforward research can be when a mooter selects appropriate terms with which to undertake their research. It also shows how important it is to carefully analyse your selected sources and appreciate how they inform each ground of appeal.

ARGUMENT CONSTRUCTION

This is the final stage you will need to engage in prior to presenting your arguments. In order to develop your skeleton, make sure you remember the following:

- your overarching argument
- to develop your argument through submissions
- to draft in a concise and professional way that links your arguments with authorities.

You should also refresh your memory about our preliminary considerations for constructing a skeleton argument on page 29.

CONSTRUCTING YOUR SKELETON ARGUMENTS IN MURRAY V JOKKER

Once you have refreshed your memory, carry out the following steps:

1. Articulate, in writing, and using numbered bullet points, the submissions that you intend to make for each ground of appeal in relation to either the Appellant or the Respondent in **Murray v Jokker**. Do not exceed one A4 page in typed print.
2. Edit your first attempt with the aim of trying to limit your submissions to take up one half of the A4 page.
3. Edit the substance of your submissions to ensure you are citing authorities to back up your argument in each submission, and using professional language.

4. Edit the 'cosmetics' of your skeleton argument, making sure the formatting, numbering, font size and use of bold and underlining is consistent. Also ensure that the headers and footers information is correct.

Once you have carried out these steps, compare your arguments to those contained in our sample skeleton arguments on the following pages. As you do this, remember that just because we have provided skeleton arguments here, it does not mean that they provide any 'definitive' exemplars. As such, when comparing skeleton arguments that you draft with those provided below, you should keep in mind a number of points: The first of these is the most important:

- There is no **right** skeleton argument that is being sought here.
  If your skeleton argument differs from the ones we have provided, that does not mean that it is wrong. Once of the most exciting things about mooting is that often there can be numerous ways of pursuing arguments and grounds of appeal. There will only very rarely be one acceptable way of doing this. If your skeleton is substantially different then take a look at the different choices made and try to understand why we chose in the way we did. Perhaps ask yourself the following questions:
- Did I discount authorities or arguments that appear in the samples? If so, why?
- Did I not encounter authorities or arguments that appear in the samples? Does this mean that my research was incomplete? Should I perhaps return to this point and see whether I could have been more thorough?
- Am I using authorities in a different way? If so, how?

SUBMISSIONS FOR THE APPELLANT

IN THE SUPREME COURT OF THE UNITED KINGDOM

Murray v. Jokker

Appellant's Skeleton Argument

Senior Counsel for the Appellant shall submit:

Ground One:

1. This Court should follow the ratio of *Lloyds Bank Plc v Rosset* [1991] AC 107, which found that 'any agreement, arrangement or understanding between the parties' that property should be shared beneficially should be upheld by the Court. The requirements for a common intention constructive trust, namely an oral agreement between the parties and detrimental reliance by the Appellant are both present in the instant case.

2. Should the oral agreement be insufficient, an intention can be inferred or imputed from the parties' conduct, following *Jones v Kernott* [2011] UKSC 53. The creation of a family home and the extensive discussions between the couple should be sufficient to infer such an intention. Alternatively, the whole course of dealing between the parties can impute an intention for a shared beneficial interest common intention constructive trust.

3. In the interests of fairness and preventing unconscionability, the court should uphold the clear intentions of the parties instantly to possess a shared beneficial interest in the family home.

Junior Counsel for the Appellant shall submit:

Ground Two:

1. Following the cases of *Midland Bank Plc v Cooke* [1995] 4 All ER 562 and *Oxley v Hiscock* [2005] Fam 211, the Appellant's share should be quantified by reference to the whole course of dealing between the parties. When looking at 'all conduct which throws light on the question of what shares were intended', as in *Midland Bank*, it is clear that the share of 50 per cent is a fair one.

2. *Stack v Dowden* [2007] 2 AC 432 and *Jones v Kernott* 2011] UKSC 53 further recognised that the 'whole course of dealing' is a broad concept, particularly in the domestic context; 'many more factors than financial contributions may be relevant to divining the

parties true intentions'. The nature of the relationship together with their conversations show the parties' intentions for there to be an equal division of assets.

3. In the interests of fairness, the law in this area requires reform to recognise the prevalence of cohabitation and ensure similar rights for cohabitation as those when a marriage breaks down. *See* **Law Commission, Cohabitation: The Financial Consequences of Relationship Breakdown, Law Com No. 307.**

The Appellant respectfully requests that this appeal be allowed.

Senior Counsel: Dr Scarlett McArdle **Junior Counsel:** Dr Sarah Cooper

SUBMISSIONS FOR THE RESPONDENT

IN THE SUPREME COURT OF THE UNITED KINGDOM

Murray v. Jokker

Respondent's Skeleton Argument

Senior Counsel for the Respondent shall submit:

Ground One:

1. *Jones v Kernott* **[2011] UKSC 53** and *Stack v Dowden* **[2007] UKHL 17** both uphold the principle that the name(s) entered on the legal title to a property should be presumed to accurately reflect equitable interests. There is nothing in the present case to rebut such a presumption. There exists no agreement to share the beneficial interest, nor any detrimental reliance on the part of the Appellant.

2. There is nothing in the actions of the parties that allow the court to objectively infer an intention to share the beneficial interest in the property, nor is it the role of the Court to impute an intention.

3. 'Equity follows the law' and fairness would not be served if the legal interests of the parties were simply ignored in the instant case.

Junior Counsel for the Respondent shall submit:

Ground Two:

1. Should a common intention constructive trust be implied or inferred here, the application of the principles in *Oxley v Hiscock* **[2005] Fam 211** shows that any beneficial interest should be reflective of the scale of contributions and in this case that would not amount to 50 per cent interest.

2. *Jones v Kernott* **[2011] UKSC 53** and *Stack v Dowden* **[2007] UKHL 17** established that in cases where a property is in a sole name, the onus rests on the non-owner to show any interest and that any quantification must be reflective of what the parties actually intended rather than what the court considers to be 'fair'. Here, it is clear that no such equal division was intended.

3. Any fair and just reform of the law to address beneficial interests in property is not feasible by means of the common law due to the diverse range of domestic circumstances that are now

encountered. *See* **Law Commission, Sharing Homes: A Discussion Paper, Law Com. 278**. Any reform should take place solely by act of Parliament.

The Respondent respectfully requests that this appeal be dismissed.

Senior Counsel: Dr Scarlett McArdle **Junior Counsel:** Dr Sarah Cooper

THINKING AHEAD AND BEING CRITICAL

Once your submissions are drafted, you must start to think critically about your argument. This involves thinking ahead to what sorts of questions the judge might ask you during the course of your moot. The two concepts are closely related because the judge will seek to clarify and test your arguments.

General questions about each ground of appeal

This section considers some general questions a judge could ask both mooters about this appeal. These questions are designed to get you thinking about both some of the broader legal concepts related to this appeal, and about how certain facts could be of concern to a judge. For each question, consider if you can articulate appropriate answers. All questions have been drawn from the grounds of appeal and show how judges are often seeking to probe mooters on their interpretation and application of legal principles. You should always be sure that you are able to express foundational principles clearly and confidently and this will stand you in good stead for any difficult questions that arise in this regard.

Ground One

What are the requirements for a common intention constructive trust?

Can we really see any form of detrimental reliance on the part of Ms Murray?

Would a resulting trust be relevant for consideration here?

What intentions can be drawn from the behaviour of the parties?

Is it appropriate for the court to 'impute' rather than 'infer' an intention here?

Where does the burden lie for showing that Ms Murray has an equitable interest here?

Could you provide a summary of the case of Jones v Kernott?

Ground Two

What is the test for determining quantification of interest in a common intention constructive trust?

Where do we find the authority for quantifying interest in a common intention constructive trust?

Would fairness here really imply a share of 50 per cent when Ms Murray provided so much less in monetary contributions?

Surely the scale of contributions would imply a much lesser share than 50 per cent?

What are the consequences for this ground of review if the court finds against Ms Murray on ground one?

If this court takes a broad approach in its interpretation of the 'whole course of dealing' then do we not run the risk of going too far?

Is it the place of this court to engage in a rewriting of the law in this area? Should this perhaps be left to Parliament?

SUMMARY

It is always important for mooters to be familiar with the broader legal concepts relevant to their ground of appeal. It is also important that they have a detailed knowledge of the cases cited in the moot problem question and in the skeleton arguments, so they are able to make use of the cases to answer judicial questions. Mooters should also spend time anticipating what questions a judge might ask about specific facts in the case, or any hypothetical scenarios the judge might ask the advocate to consider.

CONCLUSION

In this chapter, we have shown you how to analyse, research and construct an argument in relation to the moot problem presented by the fictitious case of **Murray v Jokker**. If you have engaged in the chapter and worked alongside our examples, then you have now followed the process of preparing for a moot!

6 PREPARING FOR ADVOCACY

INTRODUCTION

This book has focused on ways you can analyse, research and construct moot problems and arguments. The rationale for this being that if you do these 'front-end' tasks accurately and comprehensively, you will have the best possible platform from which to build a successful moot performance when you take to your feet as an advocate.

It would be amiss for any book on mooting to ignore the importance of oral advocacy. As such, this chapter provides guidance on five areas related to oral advocacy that, in our experience, students worry about.

PRESENTATION STYLE

Everyone has their own presentation style. An advocate's style is developed over time, but you should keep in mind the following as you practise your advocacy.

DICTION

Diction is your choice and use of words while speaking. Make sure you use words and phrases in their proper context. If you are finding a word particularly challenging to pronounce (which is not uncommon in the world of the legalese – for example, one of our students once had to use the word 'impecuniosity' throughout a moot), practise saying it – don't just ignore it or reconcile yourself to pronouncing it incorrectly. Also make sure that you know what every word you use means. Students can often get caught out using words or phrases they have seen in a judgment or law journal, which, when asked, they are not sure of the meaning of. For example, if you use a famous phrase – such as 'crosses the Rubicon' – make sure you know what the Rubicon is and who used the phrase first! Finally, beware of muddling common mooting words. For example, 'precedent' can often become 'president' when students are in the throes of advocacy. When practising, ask your colleagues to look out for these things so you can correct them.

PACE

A moderate pace is essential. Don't go too quick, or too slow! The judge needs to be able to hear your argument clearly. The most common problem is for students, often propelled by nerves, to speak too quickly. To resolve this problem, arrange with your mooting partner to give you a sign in the event you speak too quickly. For example, they could slide a post-it note with the words 'slow down' into your line of sight on the desk. You should also make sure you keep an eye on the judge; it is often fairly easy to see when you are losing a judge through speaking too quickly. Always remember that your moot performance should be a dialogue with the judge; a very formal conversation. You must respond to the judge's oral and non-verbal communications. For example, if the judge is reading, don't move on until they indicate they are ready to proceed.

VOICE AND VOLUME

A moderate volume is essential. Don't shout, or whisper! The judge must be able to hear you. Be sure to use a volume that takes account of your setting, including how close the judge is to you, how big the room is and whether or not microphones are in use. The important thing is to *use* your voice; avoid being monotone. For example, when advocating an important point raise or deepen your voice slightly, or when dealing with a sensitive issue soften your voice. Use a slightly different voice when quoting from legal authorities too, simply to distinguish the words of others from yours. These things make your performance more entertaining and encourage the judge to stay interested in your arguments.

Also, don't be overly concerned about having any particular accent – everyone has one! The important thing is that your accent can be understood, and that is achieved by using appropriate pace, volume, voices and diction. In fact, an accent can be an endearing feature for all advocates, especially if they use it to their advantage.

EYE CONTACT

Keeping eye contact with the judge is crucial. You must engage with your audience and hold their attention. Often the position of a student's notes can impact the amount of eye contact they give the judge. For example, be mindful of putting your notes on the desk, as your eyes will naturally be drawn downwards towards them. Holding paper in both hands at eye level equally draws your eyes towards the paper and not the judge. We encourage students to cradle their notes in a ring-binder folder, which can be held to their side. This way students merely side glance to the folder when they need to consult their notes. You may also find utilising a lectern beneficial as this allows your notes to be at eye level. It also looks more 'neat' and professional.

PERSONALITY

Persuasive advocates tend to be likeable and have just the right amount of confidence. Be sure to smile and use humour, as and when it is appropriate to do so. Personality makes a moot 'come to life' so don't be afraid to let yours shine through.

NON-VERBAL COMMUNICATION

In a moot, your non-verbal communication (NVC) can be just as influential as your verbal communication. NVC relates to messages your physical movements convey. We have come across lots of different NVC traits. These include over-using or using exaggerated hand movements, swaying, foot-tapping, slouched postures, hair touching and profuse sweating.

Everyone has their own nervous behaviour; the key is to be aware of what yours are and find ways to limit or remedy any that are overly distracting. For example, if you over-gesture, occupy your hands with a folder; if you touch your long hair, tie it back; if you get too hot, always bring a fresh shirt with you; and if you fidget on your feet, arrange for your mooting partner to give you a sign to make you stop.

Finally, showing the judge that you are alert to what is going on throughout the moot is an important NVC. A moot is not about a single, insular performance, but rather a collection of performances and an ongoing dialogue between all parties. Throughout a moot be sure to follow all of the arguments (not just that of your specific adversary or co-counsel), making notes, and following the mooter's and judge's use of the legal authorities in the relevant bundle. You never know when you might be called upon to answer a question or provide an authority outside of your specific performance. Never look disinterested, 'switch off' or make facial expressions during the moot that might be considered rude or contentious. Listen and remain respectful at all times.

COURTROOM ETIQUETTE

A courtroom is a very particular environment, where many unspoken and unwritten rules must be followed. There is a certain way mooters must act, speak and engage with others in a courtroom. This is known as courtroom etiquette. Becoming familiar with courtroom etiquette and using it throughout your performance should be an important feature of your presentation style. Below are some of the most common etiquette practices (outside of the obvious requirements to abide by relevant legal and ethical rules) we advise our students about.

ATTIRE

Always dress professionally. A dark suit (with a collared shirt and tie) or tailored dress (of an appropriate length) is the most typical attire in a courtroom. Avoid 'loud' colours, prints and fashion trends. It is also routine for mooters to cover up tattoos and wear only low-key jewellery and make-up.

MODES OF ADDRESS

In court, it is important that you address the people around you appropriately.

Litigants

You should refer to the parties in the moot as the Appellant or Respondent, not by any other name. Other people involved in the moot should be referred to as 'Mr X' or 'Mrs Y' where possible. If you are not given these details simply refer to people in the moot as they are labelled in the moot problem question.

Judges

Judges require different modes of address dependent upon which court they sit in. Typically, moots take place in the Court of Appeal or the Supreme Court. In these courts, judges should be referred to as Lords and Ladies. To address a male and female judge directly, you should use the phrases 'My Lord' and 'My Lady' respectively. To address them indirectly, you should use the phrases 'Your Lordship' and 'Your Ladyship'.

Trial judges should be referred to directly as 'Your Honour'. If you are referring to a trial judge's earlier ruling in a higher court, you should refer to them as 'His/Her Honour Judge Jones'.

Also be mindful that you use the correct mode of address for a judge when quoting them from a judgment. You should be aware what certain acronyms in judgments mean. For example, 'MR' and 'LJ' stand for Master of the Rolls and Lord/Lady Justice respectively.

Counsel

Co-counsel and opposing counsel are typically referred to as 'my learned friend'. This can take various forms, such as 'my learned colleague' or 'my learned friend for the opposition'.

USEFUL PHRASES

There are many phrases used by advocates that you wouldn't hear elsewhere. These include:

'May it please the court…?'
'I'm obliged my Lord/Lady…'
'Counsel for the Appellant/Respondent submits…'
'Counsel respectfully requests/submits…'
'Would the court like to be refreshed on those facts/that case…?'
'In response to my learned friend's argument, counsel submits…'
'In response to your Lordship's/Ladyship's question counsel submits…'
'Counsel for the Appellant/Respondent respectfully disagrees…'
'Counsel urges this court to…'
'As this court will know/be familiar with…'
'Your Lordship/Ladyship pre-empts counsel on that point…'
'As your Lordship/Ladyship rightfully points out…'
'Would the court find it useful if…?'

As you can see, it is common for counsel to refer to themselves in the third person. You should avoid using the words 'I' or 'We' as much as possible. This is because the court is not concerned with 'your' opinion but rather the law-based submissions you, as a legal expert, have prepared on behalf of the Appellant or Respondent, whose argument it really is. As the label suggests, the advocate is merely counsel, and not a litigant party.

You will also note that the language used is very polite and deferential to the judge and other counsel. Deference to the court is essential. You should follow and respond to the instructions of the judge as closely as possible, and always respect the submissions of other counsel. To that end, there are always certain types of phrases that you are best to avoid. Examples include:

'I think/feel/guess ...'
'He/she/you are wrong.'
'I've not bothered/thought about ...'
'I don't care ...'

It is not that the meaning of these phrases is banned from being conveyed in a moot, it is just that you must approach them euphemistically.

USING AND PRONOUNCING AUTHORITIES

Asking to use legal (and other) authorities correctly and pronouncing them correctly is an important part of courtroom etiquette.

In previous chapters, we have come across many different forms of authorities. Below we outline how you would both ask to use and pronounce some of the most common types of authorities orally.

CASE LAW

When referring to case law, you should use phrases such as, 'May counsel refer the court to the case of ...' or 'If I may refer the court to ...' You should ask the court if they wish to be refreshed with a summary of the case. You should also point out what court the case was held in and whether it is binding on the instant court, or to what extent the court should find it persuasive. You should always ask permission to use non-binding case law, especially that which emanates from a foreign jurisdiction.

Below are a number of cases we have used in earlier chapters. Beneath each case citation we provide an example of how you would pronounce the case orally.

R v Jones (Kenneth Henry) [1990] 1 WLR 1057
'The Crown against Jones, which can be found in the first volume of the Weekly Law Reports, starting at page 1057 of the year 1990.'

Attorney General's Reference (No. 1 of 1992), [1993] 1 WLR 274
'Attorney General's Reference case number 1 for the year 1992. This case can be found in the first volume of the Weekly Law Reports, starting at page 274 for the year 1993.'

Von Hannover v Germany, **Appl No 40660/08 and 60641/08 [2012] 55 EHRR 15**

'Von Hannover against Germany, a case heard by the Grand Chamber of the European Court of Human Rights, which can be found in the fifty-fifth volume of the European Human Rights Reports, starting at page 15 in 2012.'

Douglas v Hello! Ltd (No. 1) **[2001] 2 All ER 289**

'Douglas against Hello! Ltd, case number 1, which can be found in the second volume of the All England Law Reports, starting at page 289 in the year 2001.'

Once you have provided a full length citation to a case, you may ask the court to use a shorter title for the remainder of your moot performance.

LEGISLATION (DOMESTIC)

It is the task of the judge to interpret legislation. Legislation must also be introduced to the court in a courteous way – for example, by saying 'If I may refer the court to the relevant legislation...' or 'the provision the court must interpret instantly can be found in the...' Below are legislative provisions we have used in earlier chapters. Beneath each provision we provide an example of how you would pronounce the provision orally.

Criminal Attempts Act 1981 s1 (1)

'The Criminal Attempts Act of 1981, section one, sub-section 1.'

Human Rights Act 1998, s3

'The Human Rights Act 1998, section three.'

LAW COMMISSION REPORTS

You must ask permission to refer to the work of the Law Commission, and in doing so you must know the general context and impact of the Law Commission's work. For example, has Parliament followed the Law Commission's recommendations or not? What was the impetus for the Law Commission's review?

Below are reports we have used in earlier chapters. Beneath each report we provide an example of how you would pronounce it orally.

Liability for Psychiatric Illness, Law Com. 249 (1998)

'Law Commission Report number 249, a 1998 report titled liability for psychiatric illness.'

Murder, Manslaughter and Infanticide, Law Com. 304 (2009)

'The 2009 report is titled murder, manslaughter and infanticide and it is Law Commission report number 304.'

JOURNAL ARTICLES

You must ask permission to refer to the work of scholars as, while such work may be beneficial to an argument, it is not binding. In asking for permission, you must know the expertise of the scholar, what their professional role is and where, and how revered they are in their discipline. For example, what is their area of expertise? Where do they work? What is their title? Has a court referred to them before? You must also understand the generally accepted quality of the journal or book you are referring to. For instance, is it a peer-reviewed law journal or a trade magazine? You should never bring an authority before the court without being prepared to explain why the court should give it any due regard.

Below are journal articles we have used in earlier chapters. Beneath each article we provide an example of how you would pronounce it orally.

Richard Hooley, *Controlling contractual direction*, (2013) 72(1) CLJ 65

'This article was written by Professor Richard Hooley, titled controlling contractual discretion and published in 2013 in the Cambridge Law Journal, volume 72, edition 1, pages 65 to 90.'

Donal Nolan, *Horrifying events and their consequences: clarifying the operation of the Alcock criteria*, (2014) 30(3) PN 176

'This is a case note written by Professor Donal Nolan, titled horrifying events and their consequences: clarifying the operation of the Alcock criteria, published in Professional Negligence in 2014, pages 176 to 179.'

USING BUNDLES

Bundles are crucial tools for mooters. Bundles are simply the folders that a mooter's authorities are filed in. A bundle can be prepared for a single mooter or a team. You must learn to handle and navigate the bundle efficiently and effectively. To do this, we recommend the following:

- Bundles should look professional. Don't use tatty folders or folders that are too small to hold all of the authorities you need.
- Use dividers to separate the authorities clearly and number them.

- Tab the pages that you wish to quote from during the course of your argument.
- Provide clear directions to the judge, signalling the relevant tab, page number and passage of text you wish to quote from.
- Highlight (in a standard highlight colour) passages of text that you wish to quote. However, be mindful some judges prefer not to have their bundle highlighted. Always ask the judge at the point you swap your skeleton argument what their preference is.
- Prepare bundles in accordance with the rules of the relevant competition. However, whether the rules require it or not, always prepare a bundle for the judge.
- Make sure the judge's bundle is an exact replica of your own.
- Include the moot problem question and your skeleton argument at the start of the bundle.
- Mark the bundle clearly, stating your university name and which litigant you are representing.

HANDLING DIFFICULT SITUATIONS

There are a number of difficult situations that can occur during a moot. The key is to recognise when they are occurring and respond to them in an effective way. Below we provide you with some guidance on how to handle common difficult situations.

HOSTILE JUDICIAL INTERVENTION/NOT KNOWING THE ANSWER TO THE JUDGE'S QUESTION

Sometimes a judge can come across as hostile in his or her questioning style, perhaps by asking abstract questions or peppering the mooter with constant questions, or refusing to hear a particular submission. Also, occasionally, you will be asked a question you do not know the answer to. In such situations, the course of action is the same: be polite (yet firm) and redirect the judge to your submissions. If the judge is adamant he or she does not want to hear a certain submission, follow their instruction and skip it, but always look out for avenues to redirect them to it, if you think it would be useful in answering any of their questions. It is acceptable to inform a judge that you do not know the answer to a question, but you must do so confidently by redirecting them to your arguments. For example, 'Forgive me my Lord/Lady but I did not investigate that question in my research. Counsel for Appellant/Respondent submits the key issues are those outlined in our submissions...' You need to be sure that you follow a judge in their reasoning though; if they do not want to hear a submission then you should leave it, in spite of the amount of work you may have done on it!

RUNNING OUT OF TIME

Moots are strictly time controlled. You should always investigate the time limits of the mooting competition and, in particular, confirm whether judicial intervention is included in your time allowance, as this will dictate how you plan to deliver your submissions. Most moots will provide counsel with time warnings and you must keep a look-out for them. If you see that you are running out of time, do not gabble through the rest of your submissions. Instead, acknowledge to the judge that your time is limited and ask permission to simply summarise the remaining parts of your argument. This is when knowing your arguments inside out is most useful as it will allow you to summarise your points so that you at least express your argument in some form.

JUDICIAL ERROR

Sometimes a judge may make an error in relation to a legal principle or the facts of an issue. In such circumstances, you must correct the court. As always the key is to tackle the issue courteously. For example, you could use phrases such as 'My Lord/Lady forgive me, but I believe the facts are actually that...' or 'My Lord/Lady, counsel's reading of the principle is that ... not that...'

STRUGGLING COLLEAGUE

Mooting is about team-work just as much as it is about individual effort. If you see that your co-counsel is struggling, help them out in a subtle way. If their voice is drying up, pour them a glass of water. If they can't find an authority in the bundle, provide them directions. If their pen drops to the floor, pick it up. If they don't know the answer to a judge's question but you do, quietly indicate that to them and have them ask the judge permission to confer with you. As suggested above, as a team you should prearrange signals you can give to each other in the event various difficulties arise.

MISMATCHING ARGUMENTS

Sometimes your arguments will not marry up to the opposing side's arguments. This tends to mean that you have approached the ground of appeal from different angles. You will tend to know if this is the case a few days before the moot, when skeleton arguments are swapped between the two teams. This eventuality does not mean – automatically – you have made an error or your whole argument is useless. All you need to do is review the opposing team's arguments carefully and figure out how they link to yours (there will always be at least a subtle link!), and be prepared to address and respond to them. Indeed, this may mean more work than you expected, but it is best to be over-prepared than not.

RULE BREACHES

Occasionally a mooting team will break competition rules. These breaches tend not to be part of a sinister strategy by a team, but rather the result of inadvertence or a lax reading of the rules. If your team has breached a rule, the best course of action is to inform the clerk to the court, and ask permission to acknowledge the breach orally to the judge (with apologies) at the start of the moot, and indicate you will follow the judge's directions on the matter. If the opposing team has broken a rule, but do not disclose they have done so, you must decide as a team whether or not the issue is significant enough for you to inform the clerk about the matter and ask them to consult the judge. As a first port of call, however – if you do think a rule has been broken – speak to the opposing team before going to the clerk or judge. It is both professional and dignified to deal with such situations amicably and in the spirit of mutual learning.

CONCLUSION

This chapter has provided guidance on five areas related to oral advocacy that, in our experience, students worry about. Review them carefully every time you prepare to practise your advocacy. Find ways to practise that work for you – speak in front of a mirror, record your performances on audio and listen back, perform in front of friends, family, colleagues and tutors. Comprehensive preparation and practice nearly always result in successful advocacy. Good luck!

INDEX

absolute right 117
acceptance 142
acquisition 146, 148, 149, 152, 156
actus reus 10, 15, 19, 20, 21, 22, 32, 33, 36, 38, 39
alternative argument 23, 49, 52, 138
apply 8, 9, 13, 15, 23, 24, 27, 37, 38, 41, 58, 59, 68, 76, 80, 92, 99, 107, 110, 112, 115, 118, 149, 152
Article 8, 93, 94, 96, 97, 100, 107, 109, 111, 112, 114, 118
Article 10, 94, 95, 98, 111, 112, 114, 115, 119
attempt 10, 13, 19, 20, 21, 22, 33, 36, 42
attempted murder 2, 3, 4, 5, 6, 7, 8, 9, 10, 11, 12, 13, 15, 16, 17, 20, 23, 24, 25, 26, 27, 31, 32, 34, 35, 36, 38, 39, 40, 42, 71
attire 176
Attorney General 16, 22, 31, 38, 39, 42, 178
automatic resulting trust 154

bad faith 123, 129, 137, 139, 142, 144
BAIILI 14
balancing rights 102, 107, 112, 117
beneficial interest 148, 149, 152, 156, 159, 160, 162, 167, 169
beneficiaries 154

benefit 123, 124, 125, 127, 128, 129, 132, 132, 133, 134, 138, 139, 141, 143, 154
bilateral contract 128
bound 3, 24, 25, 42, 47, 69, 83, 116, 123, 150
breach 90, 92, 93, 97, 98, 103, 104, 105, 109, 112, 113, 118, 126, 131, 133, 134, 136, 139, 144, 160, 183
breach of confidence 98, 118
bundles 175, 180–1, 182
bystander 66, 73, 74, 75, 80, 82

Chancery Division 69, 148
charges 3, 42, 87
civil partner 46, 49, 50, 51, 55, 56, 65, 73, 75, 82, 105, 106
claimant 52, 61, 64, 65, 66, 67, 68, 69, 70, 77, 103, 104, 105, 106, 135
close tie of love and affection 47, 48, 50, 56, 60, 61, 65, 73, 74, 75, 82
cohabitation 157, 161, 168
common intention 148, 159, 161, 167, 169, 170, 171
common law 8, 13, 27, 31, 35, 58, 61, 71, 105, 168
confidential information 98
conscience 159
consideration 123, 125, 126, 127, 128, 129, 130, 131, 132, 133, 134, 137, 138, 140, 141, 142, 143, 153

constructive trust 153, 154, 160, 161, 167, 169, 170, 171
Council of Europe 92, 117
course of dealing 149, 159, 163, 164, 167, 171
Court of Appeal 2, 5, 20, 21, 22, 23, 46, 47, 48, 51, 52, 62, 66, 67, 68, 80, 87, 89, 90, 97, 102, 103, 111, 123, 124, 125, 126, 127, 128, 129, 130, 134, 149, 150, 152, 162, 176
cumulative argument 87, 88, 93

damages 51, 68, 69, 105
defence 2, 3, 4, 5, 6, 7, 8, 13, 17, 18, 24, 25, 26, 27, 31, 34, 35, 36, 39, 40, 42, 43, 71
defendant 3, 20, 21, 22, 23, 25, 26, 31, 33, 35, 38, 42, 77, 115
derogated 117
detriment 128, 132, 138, 143
detrimental reliance 167, 169, 170
diction 173–4
direct intent 10, 15, 32
distinguish/distinguishable 31, 42, 68, 73, 74, 81, 82, 111, 118, 124, 129, 131, 134, 141, 150
dualist system 92
duress 2, 3, 4, 5, 6, 7, 8, 9, 11, 12, 13, 15, 17, 18, 23, 24, 25, 26, 27, 31, 34, 35, 36, 39, 40, 42, 43, 71, 123, 124, 125, 126, 127, 129, 130, 131, 132, 134, 135, 136, 137, 139, 140, 141, 142, 144, 153
duress of threats 12, 13

economic duress 123, 124, 125, 126, 127, 129, 130, 131, 132, 134, 135, 136, 137, 139, 140, 141, 142, 144, 153

equitable interest 149, 152, 153, 154, 155, 156, 158, 159, 161, 162, 163, 169, 170
equity 147, 153, 154, 169
etiquette 176–8
European Court of Human Rights 107, 111, 116, 117, 119, 179
existing duty 132
express trust 162
eye contact 174–5

fairness 149, 150, 151, 152, 154, 156, 159, 167, 168, 169, 171
foreign jurisdiction 178
foreseeable 66, 73, 77, 78, 80, 83
freedom of contract 130
freedom of expression 94, 96, 98, 102, 103, 105, 106, 107, 114

good faith 130, 131, 137
Grand Chamber 112, 118, 179

held on trust 154
High court 48, 69, 86, 89, 96, 148, 152
Hillsborough 56, 57, 65
House of Lords 24, 25, 31, 39, 40, 42, 47, 61, 64, 65, 78, 80, 81, 83, 84, 103, 108, 148, 161, 162, 176
human rights 91–2, 93, 95, 96, 97, 98, 99, 100, 101, 102, 103, 104, 105, 106, 107, 111, 112, 114, 116–17, 119, 153, 179
hypothetical 145, 171

illegitimate pressure 130, 131
immediate aftermath 57, 60, 64, 67, 76, 80
imputed 148, 159, 167
inferred intention 167, 168, 169
intention 5, 10, 11, 15, 16, 22, 34,

35, 38, 142, 148, 149, 150, 155, 156, 159, 160, 161, 164, 167, 169
interests of fairness 157, 165, 168, 169, 170, 171
international treaty 92, 116

judges 4, 35, 39, 42, 148, 170, 176–7, 181
judges questions 42, 181–3
judicial error 182
judicial intervention 181–2
jury directions 3, 8, 9, 12, 23, 32, 34

Law Commission 14, 19, 26–7, 31, 40, 42, 43, 84, 161, 164, 168, 179–80
learned friend 177
legal title 158, 162, 164, 169
legislation 14, 19, 58, 92, 99, 132, 155, 179; *see also* statute
litigants 176

margin of appreciation 98, 103, 117
media 46, 55, 57, 86, 96, 113
mens rea 10, 15, 19, 33, 36, 38
merely preparatory 10, 15, 19, 21, 22, 30, 31, 36, 38, 42
misdirect 4, 32, 34
mismatch in arguments 182–3
mode of address 176–7
mortgage 148, 158, 160, 161, 162, 163
murder 8, 18, 23, 24, 26, 27, 31, 32, 34, 35, 36, 39, 40, 180

negligence 51, 52, 56, 60, 62, 68, 69, 180
nervous shock 47, 50, 52, 54, 55, 56, 57, 59, 65, 73
non-verbal communication 174

obiter dicta 24, 25, 39
objective 118, 130, 148, 159, 169
offer 138, 141, 142
oral agreement 167
original intention 159
overrule 8, 40, 124, 129, 131, 155

pace 174
parliament 27, 31, 40, 42, 43, 65, 68, 92, 105, 170, 171, 179
parliamentary sovereignty 92
permission 178, 179, 180, 182, 183
personality 64, 175
policy 26, 33, 40, 74
polite 39, 177, 181
practical benefit 123, 124, 125, 127, 128, 129, 134, 138, 141, 143
precedent 3, 8, 24, 25, 26, 27, 29, 31, 39, 40, 42, 47, 74, 79, 87, 123, 150, 174
presentation 43, 84, 119, 140, 173–5, 176
presumed resulting trust 154
presumption 74, 75, 82, 158, 162, 169
primary victim 64, 65, 67, 74, 75, 80, 82, 83
principle of fairness 150, 151
privacy 86, 87, 88, 89, 92, 93, 94, 96, 97, 99, 100, 101, 102, 103, 104, 105, 106, 107, 109, 110, 111, 112, 113, 114, 118
promise 123, 124, 128, 129, 133, 134, 138
pronunciation 178–80
property 21, 123, 148, 154, 158, 160, 161, 162, 163, 164, 167, 169
proximity 48, 49, 50, 52, 55, 57, 60, 61, 62, 64, 65, 66, 67, 68, 70, 76, 77, 78, 80, 81, 83

psychiatric damage 54, 56, 57, 59, 74; *see also* psychiatric injury, psychiatric harm

psychiatric harm 65, 66; *see also* psychiatric damage, psychiatric injury

psychiatric injury 50, 51, 60, 62; *see also* psychiatric damage, psychiatric harm

psychological harm 78, 83

PTSD 47, 48, 51, 54, 55, 56, 57

public interest 87, 88, 89, 90, 91, 94, 96, 97, 98, 99, 100, 101, 102, 103, 104, 105, 106, 108, 109, 112, 113, 114, 115, 116, 118

quantifying interest 162, 164, 171

reasonable expectation 87, 88, 89, 91, 94, 96, 97, 98, 102, 103, 104, 105, 106, 107, 108, 110, 111, 113, 114, 115, 119

reasonable person 131, 136, 142

reasonable person of ordinary sensibilities 23, 35

rebuttable presumption 73, 74, 75, 82, 159, 162

respect for private and family life 94, 95, 99, 114

resulting trust 152, 154, 159, 160, 171

rubicon 173

rule breaches 183

running out of time 182

scholarship 27, 71, 99, 132

secondary victim 47, 48, 49, 50, 51, 52, 53, 54, 55, 56, 59, 60, 61, 62, 63, 64, 65, 66, 67, 68, 71, 73, 74, 75, 78, 79, 80, 81, 82, 83, 84, 153

share ownership 148, 150, 162, 164

skeleton argument 29, 30, 32, 33, 35, 36, 37, 38, 39, 41, 42, 43, 72, 77, 79, 80, 84, 109, 110, 113, 119, 138, 140, 141, 145, 165, 167, 169, 171, 181, 183

special relationship 53, 74

stare decisis 123, 150

statute 13, 19, 92; *see also* legislation

struggling colleague 182

subjective 106, 118, 130

Supreme Court 2, 3, 5, 6, 7, 20, 21, 22, 24, 25, 30, 36, 38, 39, 47, 87, 88, 90, 91, 98, 111, 114, 123, 125, 126, 127, 128, 130, 139, 142, 148, 149, 150, 152, 158, 167, 169

team 2, 14, 29, 127, 180, 182, 183

tort 45, 46, 51, 52, 57, 59, 61, 62, 152, 156; *see also* tortious

tortious 48, 51; *see also* tort

treaty incorporation 93, 117

trial court 7

trial judge 4, 6, 8, 9, 25, 32, 34, 176

trust 55, 153, 154, 159, 160, 161, 162, 167, 169, 171

unaided senses 60, 61, 64

unconscionable 159, 160

undue influence 163

unilateral contract 128–9, 130

variation of contract 130, 131, 136

vitiate 130, 136, 144

voice 174, 182

volume 174

whole course of dealing 149, 159, 163, 164, 167, 171

yardstick of fairness 149, 152, 156